I AM: This One Life

Carlos Alvarez Cotera

BALBOA.
PRESS
A DIVISION OF HAY HOUSE

Balboa Press books may be ordered through booksellers or by contacting:

Balboa Press
A Division of Hay House
1663 Liberty Drive
Bloomington, IN 47403
www.balboapress.com
1 (877) 407-4847

Because of the dynamic nature of the Internet, any web addresses or links contained in this book may have changed since publication and may no longer be valid. The views expressed in this work are solely those of the author and do not necessarily reflect the views of the publisher, and the publisher hereby disclaims any responsibility for them.

The author of this book does not dispense medical advice or prescribe the use of any technique as a form of treatment for physical, emotional, or medical problems without the advice of a physician, either directly or indirectly. The intent of the author is only to offer information of a general nature to help you in your quest for emotional and spiritual well-being. In the event you use any of the information in this book for yourself, which is your constitutional right, the author and the publisher assume no responsibility for your actions.

The author and fine artist, Carlos Alvarez Cotera, created book cover and dog portrait paintings.
artcotera.com

Print information available on the last page.

ISBN: 978-1-5043-7919-9 (sc)
ISBN: 978-1-5043-7920-5 (hc)
ISBN: 978-1-5043-7929-8 (e)

Library of Congress Control Number: 2017906050

Balboa Press rev. date: 04/26/2017

Introduction

I am more than the person I had thought myself to be for the past fifty years. I have come to learn that I am not alone, I have come to believe I have a partner that has been with me since birth and even before, in fact, we have been together since the beginning of my journey many lifetimes ago. This partner is within me, a part of me, a larger part of me actually, a part of all that has ever been before, all that is and all that will ever be. It is the energy some have called soul, spirit, source or even God. The name is not important but recognizing the existence of it is crucial to the understanding of life. I admit it is not easy to accept this concept which makes so much sense to me now, I only ask that you follow me on this journey with the hope that you too will come to the same realization I have come to. At the very least I hope you will find this book to be a good read or perhaps even find some of its content to be beneficial.

For so long I have listened to the different explanations given for the creation of life, the religious teachings, the evolution theory, the many interpretations that have existed all throughout history regarding all of them and the fervor with which men have tried to push their ideology on others, in many cases to try and control the masses for their own benefit. The answers to the questions about the meaning of life have been grossly distorted and in the attempt to explain this great mystery, a myriad of interpretations have abounded. I believe that all the guidance we need is within us at all times no matter who you are, where you are from or what you believe in, we all have the same innate wisdom.

The perfection that we are is so amazing and so simple to experience and understand that looking back I think, how did I not know this before? But if I had not experienced what I have experienced up until this moment I would not be here today, knowing what I have come to know. This may sound complex at first and even unbelievable but once it is put to the test and practiced it will become so natural that you will leave your past behind and you will start living the life you intended to live.

I will speak in the first person and explain from my own experience, my own knowledge and the wisdom I have received through what I consider to be my teachers. I also hope that in doing so the reader will feel more involved in the experience and every time you read "I …", something will resonate within.

I am soul, source energy and at the same time I am flesh and bones. I am physical and non-physical, this is a partnership established long ago. My soul or source energy has been before, it has been in physical and non-physical stages for a timespan that I have no exact knowledge of and I find no importance in the recollection of who I once was. In this present lifetime I am becoming, expanding, growing and evolving as I intended to before I became this human body I am today.

My purpose in life as I believe it is for all, is to enjoy the experience I am having right now upon this earth and in the process become more than I have been before. I have a guidance system that alerts me at all times and lets me know if I am on the right path or not. This source energy that flows in me, through me, and all around me, speaks to me in the form of feelings, whatever I feel at any given moment is the indicator of where I am at that precise moment.

There are only two emotions I experience no matter what the circumstances are, one feels good and the other one does not. In either case, the source within is letting me know if I am on the right path or not. When I encounter any situation or experience, I have an automatic reaction, it may be a gut feeling, a vibe or a sensation, whatever the case may be, if the emotion that I have is positive, that means I am where I am supposed to be, and when it is negative, I am not. This guidance system, which I will call Soul, knows and alerts me in the form of a feeling, and feeling is the key word I want to really get through to the reader, for this feeling is the most accurate indicator of my wellbeing. If I am in sync with Soul I will feel good and if I am in discord with Soul I will not feel good. This sounds simple enough but since I understand it may be confusing I will explain further throughout this book.

I have picked up a lot of characteristics, behaviors, beliefs, concepts and explanations along the path of whatever many years I have lived. The environment in which I was born into, the people I have encountered and those who have been part of my life at one point or another and the experiences I have had, have all conditioned me to think and behave a certain way and these patterns that I have accumulated along the way are so seeded in my mind that it seems almost impossible to sort out and discard all the possible negative influences.

In my own experience, my history in this lifetime has been so destructive, that I almost had to undergo Electroconvulsive Therapy, formerly known as Electro-Shock Therapy. A lifelong battle with depression, fear, worry and anxiety brought me to where I am today. My path made me look everywhere for answers, many professionals, from clergy, to alternative medicine and even to the occult, were tried out in search of a solution but of course, none of it brought me to the solution I was seeking. My desire to feel well; to learn about myself and to understand myself created an incessant appetite for knowledge. I see now it was not all a waste of time, it was thanks to those experiences that I was being guided all along to reach for a better and perhaps even a more spiritual existence.

I wanted so much to experience peace in my life; I sought out books on the subjects of motivation and spirituality; which felt very comforting at times. Before that, I had looked to religion for the answers to my problems with no success. It feels now like my Soul was always aware of my struggle, and it was. Soul just could not bring me out of my despair, however, it did try to and it did light some candles to show me the way along my journey.

I know now that the universe could not really help me much in the state I was in for I was creating my own torture and was therefore not able to allow wellbeing in. You see, the universe is all, everything that was, is and will ever be. It is wise, it is eternal, it is nothing but wellness and goodness. When it is said that we are all connected, it is hard to understand this concept and I at best saw it as a vague possibility. The energy that creates this immense, ever expanding universe runs through all that is, and that includes you and it also includes me. Soul, the source energy I spoke of, is part of that universe, and it has access to infinite wisdom. For a long time, probably right up until recently that all sounded like an abstract concept, a fairy tail, perhaps just something weird people would say to try to appear spiritual. Some are doing just that, with much disregard for the wellbeing of others but now I know that it is not some fable, it is not an abstract philosophy but a tangible reality, and this is why I believe it.

When I think the habitual thoughts I have in the luggage I've been carrying for fifty years, I don't feel well because my bags are filled with negative thoughts and emotions but when I put these bags down and consciously choose to focus on something that is pleasant I feel better. I have been carrying a mixed luggage, some bags are filled with good, positive things and some not so good and certainly not so positive and I open them accordingly depending on the situation I am faced with at any given time. Some of us have luggage that has mostly bad thoughts and experiences in them. It is my intention to help you in letting go of that luggage, I want you and I to put those bags down at the airport, get on a plane and leave them all behind. We are then going to buy a new set of luggage and fill them up with only good thoughts until they are full and then buy some more and fill those up as well.

I know that no one can walk in anyone's shoes, my journey is my own and it is as unique as everyone else's. If you are like me, one who has hope, one who has had glimpses of "Perhaps there's more than that which I thought was true and have experienced so far", then give me a chance to show you how your life can change as mine has. You do not have to believe you are in need of change to benefit; this wisdom can change a life that's good, bad, great or magnificent into more. For those who enjoy life as it is, it will get better and for those whose life is a Calvary, a radical change to a blissful existence is within reach.

There are thousands of ideas and beliefs regarding life; it's purpose and the right and wrong ways to live it. There are countless interpretations and there are countless ways people experience their time on earth. I intend to share with you my interpretation; which is based on my own experience. It is not my intention to discredit others or to tell you that my way is the right way for I believe that your way, the way you have chosen to live your life may very well be the right way for you. It is my hope that this book will be of help to those who see the value in it and nothing more.

CHAPTER 1

"God"

It has been such a desire of man to believe in a creator to give purpose and meaning to life that I do not know at what point in history this idea of imagining a person-like figure, male or female, was created to glorify and revere with such passion. It must have been at the point when humanity realized that the physical form was subject to decay and disintegration, that in wanting to keep the spirit alive in some form and out of fear of the unknown it was then decided.

Gods were created to bless harvests and countless other desires. Sacrifices were made to honor these Gods, rituals to attract desired events and circumstances and the list goes on. Religions later emerged, creating their own versions of these Gods in order for those in power to set rules and doctrines to control and manipulate others. Much success was achieved in this endeavor and for generations, the faithful gathered to worship and still do to this day. Needless to say, history has shown the power of these institutions, which to a large degree have done more harm than good. I will not go into the details of these negative effects, for I wish not to judge others, I simply intend on stating historic facts to make my point. I will leave it up to you to find evidence of the negative influence of religion on humanity; this should not be hard since one need only look back at its history to see it.

There have been those who have tried to convey knowledge which could free humanity of the affliction of believing in that one, all-powerful being. The wisdom spread by these seers was profound but it failed to reach a large number of people. Some were persecuted and killed at times and even their messages became distorted and misinterpreted. These extraordinary beings were so powerful in their understanding and their teachings so profound, that after thousands of years their words still inspire today. If one were to study these teachings, even when the physical experiences of these teachers where spread over many different periods throughout history, one will find that their message had much in common with each other, and the core teaching was the same.

The word God in the context that has been used for so long feels very heavy, and it is such a source of controversy that one may wonder how a word that is meant to evoke nothing but love can do so much damage and creates so much division. It is fair to say however, that there are many who do a lot of good in the name of that word as well.

I choose not to use the word for it carries too much baggage and it creates an almost automatic reaction in most people, a mental picture with a preconceived notion of the word. If I were to tell you that God is not an old man with a white beard but that every old man with a white beard is God, you would probably close the book and stop reading. I would encourage you to continue on however, even when I tell you that God is you, it is I, and it is all that is.

There is no separation between men and God for that which has been called God as a particular shape or form was only a figment of someone's imagination. I therefore will replace this word with universe or source or spirit but perhaps replacing it is not an accurate statement for the universe has never harmed nor judged anyone.

It is hard for man to believe that the universe or source of life was never created. It seems that there is this intrinsic notion that everything has a beginning and an end, alternatively, if I were to ponder the idea that all is possible and infinity and immortality just are, then nothing was ever created, it just is, there was no beginning and there is no end. I want to be opened to the possibility that all of my concepts may be incorrect and in fact there are other theories that may seem foreign but that may very well be in fact the truth. Not the ultimate truth, for all truths are subject to interpretation but the truth or wisdom I am trying to convey here.

The concept of death as the dissolution of my body and the end of my life is flawed, for even when I stop being physical I still remain. Death is but a transition from physical to nonphysical form, therefore, there is no death. The question for some then becomes, where do I go? I go nowhere, I just am. The universe is endless, no space and no time. This event we call life on earth is but a projection of vibrations. It is common knowledge that everything that exists when observed with the most powerful of magnification is but vibration. Vibrations manifest into all that which we see, smell and touch. Our senses perceive and interpret everything that occurs in all of our experiences through vibrations. I know that I am energy; I know that everything is energy and energy is vibration. This knowledge is simple yet profound.

Perhaps you have felt at some point that there is something more than just existing, maybe you have sensed the famous, "it feels like I have been here before" or the well-known phenomenon called the "Deja Vu" experience. This is not my brain playing tricks on me but an experience that lets me know that I am more than a physical being, they are small glimpses of knowledge not from this physical plane.

When I look back and pay attention at events in my life, I notice that things have happened which have surprised me, things I did not expect, things I deemed as a lucky break or a coincidence just to name a few. There are those who say that everything happens for a reason or it is fate. Perhaps there are no coincidences, there is not a set destiny and God is not responsible for my good fortune nor is the Devil for my misfortune, for neither really exists in the context that is used in certain religions or belief systems. There are many atheists living wonderful fulfilling lives, as there are many devoted believers who seem to be missing out on any type of meaningful life.

Though faith is a very powerful and effective method of achieving what I want, it is not because the almighty is the granter of my wishes. When I pray I believe and trust with strong feelings that things will turn out well and as long as I do not contradict my desire with doubt the universe answers my prayers. It was my intention and desire what produced the results even if I wish to credit an outside entity. Perhaps you are skeptical of this concept, but it is my expectation that you will realize this truth in the subsequent chapters.

It is my faith and my belief that the universe gathers the necessary elements on my behalf is what produces the desired outcomes in my everyday life. I am a powerful machine with extraordinary powers, who needs only to understand and apply the laws of the universe to create the most wonderful life experience while I am in this time and space.

I once bought a rock in a store that had an inscription on it that spoke to me very strongly even though I was very young and it read, "You are not what you think you are, but what you think you are".

There will be much fear in many at the thought that there is no God, especially those whose beliefs are tied to a religious dogma. This will be so, probably mainly out of guilt since guilt is one of the main byproducts of religions such as Catholicism to give an example, but if I think about that for a minute, would a loving God wish for a negative emotion for me to experience?

Religions have created the idea of hell and once again, this is a way to keep believers in fear. All of these techniques were put in place to control and manipulate men. Would a loving, forgiving, all powerful, creator of all there is really allow for his or hers children to experience such horrors? I believe heaven and hell are not a destination, a place up in the skies or in the depth of the molting underbelly of the earth. The closest experience to a heaven or a hell is right here, right now, in my everyday existence and I decide in which I want to dwell. It is my hope that after reading this book you will choose to live in heaven, right here, right now.

After being baptized at the age of fifteen in the Catholic church, I became very involved in this religion and the fear and guilt that arose from that experience were very traumatic for me as

I am sure it was and still is for many. One day I asked myself, "if God is love", I then associated the love my mother has for me and I realized there was no possibility that God would be a punisher for my mother would not desire anything but good for me, no matter what the circumstances were. I then, from that moment on, believed there could not be a hell since a loving God would not create that for me, but at the same time I felt it would be I who would create it while in this body.

CHAPTER 2

"The Law Of Attraction"

There are many universal laws that exist and it is easy to accept and understand most of them, for example, the law of gravity. There is no doubt that when I let go of a brick I am holding out in front of me, this brick will certainly fall to the ground. The law of attraction is too a very important law and the most personal law I know of. Whatever I think and most accurately, whatever I feel, I will attract. Things, people, situations and conditions of a similar vibration will be brought together for me to experience. Without a doubt the understanding and the application of this law changed my life forever. In this chapter and throughout the book, I will try to explain this wonderful law and how it can be of benefit. I truly believe this is the most powerful law in the universe.

Man is a thinking machine, I have countless thoughts everyday and many of these thoughts are usually the same, recycled day after day, year after year, becoming a habit that after many years of practice, it is very difficult to reprogram my brain and change them in order to have a better experience but just accepting that this is so will be beneficial. Because these thoughts carry much momentum I do not expect to flick a switch and turn them off at will, I so have wished many of times that I could have. I can however begin to pay a little more attention to whatever it is I am thinking about, every day, a little bit at a time and in doing so, I will feel better and better as I consciously adjust the content of my thoughts.

Because of the law of attraction, whenever I think a thought, for example; "I feel depressed", the law of attraction will bring into my experience more thoughts, people, conditions and events that will match that thought. By the same token, if I am feeling happy, more thoughts, people, conditions and events matching that experience will also begin to come my way. I am a vibrational magnet and I get whatever I think about whether I want it or not.

In my own experience, much misery came my way. Anxiety, fear, worry and depression were my predominant emotions. People around me, most with well meaning intentions would offer advice and would tell me things such as, "snap out of it!", "you are always going to be miserable", "you should do this or that", "you are too negative", "try to think positive" and so on. This type of advice, which is really never helpful, would always make things worse and to add insult to injury I felt overwhelmed with guilt since I had no apparent reason for feeling the way I felt. I had what summed up to be all of the right components to be a happy person, of course, that did not matter for I felt the way I did anyway and since I was diagnosed with bipolar-depression I had a nice label to back up my condition. I will probably never forget the day that I was told I had created my own misery. This comment enraged me. Why would anyone create this hell for himself or herself intentionally? I felt this person had no compassion and was extremely cruel, but of course this person without knowing it was in fact right. I did create the life I was living, not because I wanted to but because I did not know better. I do now.

The trick to changing my life around is to change one thought at a time, and even if at first I am not able to catch all of the thoughts that pour in constantly, just being easy on myself is the best first step. Judging and blaming myself for not being able to accomplish something no matter what the subject is, is contradictory to my intention to feel better. When I become aware a thought I am having is negative I will take a moment and stop the thought before it grows larger and gains momentum. I will guide my thinking towards a different subject. For example, if I catch myself saying, "I feel down, this sucks, I am never going to get better", I will stop myself and focus on something else. This could be as simple as just playing with my dog, going for a walk, or taking a bath. Perhaps the most effective way to achieve a better state of mind is simply by focusing on my breathing. I will pay attention to my breath; I will feel the air going in and out, over and over again. I have found this to be a very effective method to stop the thoughts and it has great potential to bring me into a better feeling place.

"I think, therefore I am", a famous quote that was revolutionary in its time. Some have declared this idea to be flawed but there may be some validity to this statement as in the engraved rock I mentioned earlier. I am what I think about, I am who I am today because of the thoughts I have thought right up until this moment. Thoughts are very powerful and the power lies in the emotions that follow them. A feeling follows most thoughts, this feeling, as I mentioned before is my inner source or Soul letting me know if the thought I am having right now is good for me or if it is not. Let's say, I am watching a video of puppies playing. For most people, an emotion will immediately arise which will be pleasant and calming. Soul would be in accord with this feeling and therefore I will be feeling good. If I instead am walking in the park, enjoying a beautiful day and I hear a loud barking coming towards me, my thoughts then would not be pleasant and I would feel fear under this conditions. I am on my own sort of speak in that example for Soul would feel not such thing as fear and that is because the universe is only goodness and wellness and nothing that diverts from that would bring me feelings that do not feel good. This guidance system lets me know whether I am in sync with source or I am not. The truth is that I created the puppies and I also created the dog attack. Had I not brought them into my reality by way of thoughts and emotions, which I had been experiencing consciously or not, I would not have experienced either. The way I feel lets me know if I will need to focus better in the future or not. As I become more in sync with Soul I will not have the negative experiences again.

In order to understand this, I need to start at the beginning. I was source energy before I came into this body, as non-physical I looked upon the world and I decided I would choose where I am going to be born and even who my parents are going to be. It is said that groups of souls travel together from lifetime to lifetime, this would explains the affinity or discord I feel when I meet others, there are many times I sense or feel a vibe I cannot explain. It is this feeling that we have met before and even though I do not know when or how nor do I know under which circumstances we have interacted before, that vibe is in fact telling me that we have shared a moment in time. There are no coincidences and I do not meet people by chance. No matter how brief my exchange with others is, there is a purpose and this is the universe bringing us together in a wonderful creative dance. Many will disagree with this premise since they would not have chosen the people and or environment in their lives that have caused so many negative outcomes for them but that is only a perception in the absence of the knowledge Soul has. It is ignorance of this knowledge that has been brought forth that makes it feel this way. I experienced this absence of Soul for fifty years and it felt very lonely.

Allow me to play with this theory for a moment. I come into my body as a baby knowing I chose this time and place for the opportunity it provided for my own development and that of the universe. I want to continue the journey from my previous lifetime and grow and evolve to more than I have been before. I also came because I wanted to enjoy and rejoice amongst the people and world of these times. As a child, my intention is to have fun and to enjoy my time here. I am aware that I will encounter many of situation, events, people and conditions, some of which will feel good and some that will not but I know that I am not alone. I have that other part of me that is wise, it knows all that I have lived before, It knows my personality, it knows I have value, it knows I am loved, it knows that I can have, do and be whatever I desire. My Soul knows that when I am in sync with it everything is magical and the universe is behind me, and together we will create wonderful things and in all of this process I will experience joy.

As I grow older and experiences begin, the happy and joyful child I was is exposed to others, and these others begin to mold and manipulate my development. There are many of teachings imposed upon me, many situations affect the development of this child and later youth until I am finally old enough and I am able to be that which I was meant to be. By this time I have accumulated some baggage, I am starting to carry bags I have picked up along the way. I seem to have no knowledge of a partner; it feels like I am on my own and with plenty of questions. However, as I look back at the journey thus far, I can see there have been signs along the way, some guidance, some experiences and people that have crossed my path who have influenced who I think I am now. All of these events that have happened up until this moment, whatever this moment is for the me right now, had to have happened for me to have picked up this pen to write this book. I believe that it is not by chance that I am writing it.

So I am here, I have thoughts, I have emotions, I have beliefs and I have knowing. My thoughts are interpretation of events and circumstances. I have come to these thoughts via the influence of others and also by my own conclusions, opinions and interpretations on all subjects. These thoughts can be help or hindrance and how I handle these thoughts determines what kind of life I will experience. A psychologist once told me, "You have a very messed up view of the world", and he was right.

Emotions are tied directly to thoughts. At times it may seem that my emotion or feelings precede my thoughts, but that is only because they have become so automatic and habitual. So many thoughts that seem to come at the same time that I am so overwhelmed I do not recognize that the thought was there before the emotion. Thought, emotion, thought, emotion, thought, emotion, so many that the order gets tangled up at times. I have so many thoughts in the course of the day that it is probably hard to pinpoint one out at any given time. They have such momentum that the pattern repeats over and over again without me even realizing it is happening.

I have beliefs, and these are nothing more than thoughts that I have practiced so often and for so long that they are now what

I call a belief. A belief can be true or false and in both cases it feels very real to me, but it also can change in time depending upon my experiences. What I believed as a child growing up morphs and it sometimes becomes a completely different belief as I get older but getting older does not necessarily make the beliefs true or false. It is merely a change in perception.

I have knowing, and this is the experience or experiences that I have personally had and it is not based on second hand knowledge or the opinions of others. My knowing is my own, actual experiences that are not based on interpretation. For example, if I cut myself with a sharp blade by accident, I bleed. I also know it hurts for I experience physical pain.

So now that I have established these premises I would like the opportunity to show how life can change and how I can experience the one life I intended to have before I came into physical existence and was aware I had a partner and a universe behind me with the power to do it all. I want to change my thoughts, which in turn will change my emotions, which in turn will change my beliefs, which in turn will change my knowing, which in turn will change my life.

The first thing I need to do is relax, and this is the hardest one for me. I need to go easy on myself no matter what the circumstances are. If you are anything like me, you are one who wants to learn quickly, so that you can apply what you have learned, and focus intensely in order to achieve the goal. If this were the case, I would strongly encourage you to do the opposite. It was not until I decided not be judgmental and stop wanting to be a perfectionist that I allowed life to unfold. I tried to keep as clear mind as possible and I was then able to enjoy the unfolding. You see, it is hard to undo fifty years of thinking a certain way. I realized that the idea that I had to reprogram my mind and undo all of the mess in my head was an impossible task. I decided to approach the whole situation as if I had been born yesterday. So, if today I catch myself thinking in the old habitual ways, I would stop and say, "no, that is not for me." Whenever I recognized that the thoughts were not beneficial for me or I knew they would not make me feel good, I would consciously make the decision that I would let them pass and take a moment to veer off that pattern of thought towards something more pleasant and if I was unable to find positive thoughts, I would then become very vague in my approach and look for anything in my mind or my surroundings that would keep the thoughts away. Once I started doing this every time it happened, the less and less those thoughts came and they eventually began to be replaced by positive thoughts for my habits had transformed and had adapted to the new way of thinking. I will find whatever thoughts and actions I need to take whenever thoughts or emotions, that do not feel good, enter the picture. I will not analyze them nor will I pay attention to them for this would be a sure way of attracting more of that which I want to avoid. The moment I feel them coming, I will stop and change the circumstances.

The law of attraction works this way on my everyday life. Whenever I think a thought, other thoughts like it begin to form and head my way. Situations and conditions appear that reinforce that which I am thinking about. This is wonderful when I am thinking positive, happy thoughts for I will experience more and more of that which pleases me but when the thoughts are negative, and I will know when they are for I will feel the negativity right away, then it will not be a pleasant experience because I am now attracting more of that negativity and if I couple the thoughts with strong negative emotions, it will just get worse and once it becomes a belief, that is a sure recipe for disaster for I cannot attract good to a bad situation. I am sure you have experienced this in your lives at some point. It is said, "When it rains, it pours." Well, it does, not only does it pour but a storm is fast approaching.

I have suffered from chronic depression for most of my life. I am not aware of when or how it started. It was probably a thought, a reaction to some event or situation, then another and another, until it became a pattern. Visits to psychologists, priests and others, perpetuated the condition. So much attention was being given to my mental state that it just grew and grew to the point I was given a new label in later years of "bipolar depression." No amount of medications was enough to stop the madness. Whatever thoughts I give my attention to will become my experiences in one form or another. My distorted view of reality is nothing more than my perception or interpretation of events and circumstances that are happening in my life. The thoughts I should consciously create instead should be about the life I want to experience and not the life I currently have. That is if the life I currently have is unpleasant. I used to think that if I forced myself to think differently, if I tried to change the beliefs about what I thought was my reality, as it was suggested to me once, that I was fooling myself. I thought I would just be creating some kind of fantasy, and therefore, I would stop being myself. I thought it would be like a make-believe world, something fake, and I would rather feel bad but be myself, than good by pretending to be something I am not. I rejected this notion and therefore I continued on creating my own torture. The truth is that what I was calling reality was a screwed up perception of the world, the only reason it felt real was because I had created it and as I believed it to be real, so it was. My thoughts, emotions and beliefs built a hell on earth for me and I called it reality. Was that not in actuality the fantasy I was avoiding?

I know that when I am feeling down, when things are not going well, the last thing I want is for others to pretend to know what is best for me and for them to tell me how to get out of the hole I am in with words that sound hollow and meaningless. They are not in my shoes, they have no idea how I feel, but do I really believe that? I know there are millions of people in similar situations and they may very well know how it feels, however, their advice is only valuable once they have overcome their despair for misery cannot be of help to misery. I know from experience the guilt I felt for being depressed. I seemingly had no reason to be feeling this way, especially when I saw so many others in conditions that appeared worse than mine. However, others' experiences are not my own, and the ones that hurt are the ones I experience for no one else can feel it the same way no matter how similar they may seem to be. I now know that if I apply and practice what I am suggesting, if I just try for a short period of time, maybe a month or two, how would it hurt? I had suffered for half a century, one or two months was a walk in the park for me. For those who live in pain right now, I offer this simple strategy that has worked for me personally and I expect it will work for you as well. I mention it again purposely because by doing so I am intending to remind you of its importance.

I will pay attention to my breathing. I will pay attention to the air going in and out of my nose. This sounds simple enough but it takes much practice and concentration to achieve it successfully. I will inhale through my nose and I will feel the air going in. I will exhale through my nose and feel the air going out through my nose and I will notice the flow of air going out right up to the point when I feel I have to take another breath. When my attention is on my breathing I stop thinking, giving myself a break from the incessant chatter in my head. While doing this exercise I am aware I will have thoughts that will try to come right in and distract me, as this happens, I will not feel bad or give it any thought, I will just let it pass, I will acknowledge that the thoughts are there and consciously bring myself back to my breathing. I will do this, as many times as it takes and I will not allow any negative feelings while doing this exercise. I will just accept that it takes practice to master it.

This simple meditation technique is very useful. It interrupts my thinking pattern and allows me to connect with my inner being. I do not need to be aware of this, looking for some kind of connection defeats the purpose of quieting the mind; it happens automatically, in fact, this connection also happens every time I feel inspired, every time I am enjoying something, every time I am laughing, dancing or doing anything that makes me feel good. Whenever I find myself in a pleasant situation and I find joy in what I am doing, the energy of the universe and the source within are both there with me. I will seek out more of these experiences as much as I can. These moments are but a taste of the life I intended to live since the beginning.

When I think a thought that carries a strong emotion, its power is multiplied. Emotions or strong feelings, shorten the time needed to accomplish that which I desire, so I will make sure that at those times when my thoughts are favorable, when they feel good, that is when I want to really stay in the moment. I will feel the emotion, I will notice how good it feels and I will amplify it, I will spend as much time as possible basking in that state of mind. This joyful experience will not only help me in the moment I am experiencing it but it will also spread to every other area of my life. I therefore will try and have these experiences often.

If the emotions on the other hand do not feel good, I will change the thought and switch to something that pleases me as soon as possible. If I am unable to do this for any reason, if I become frustrated during the breathing exercise, I will try and distract myself. I will get up and take a walk, I will take a bubble bath, I will go get a massage and I will go to the park and walk the dog. I will do whatever I am able to do, in order to change the current dissatisfying experience. Events, people and circumstances are part of my life experience and I cannot avoid the ones that do not please me all of the time, but I do not have to put up with any situation nor endure negativity. Even when I cannot physically remove myself from the events, people or situations, I can choose my thoughts about the conditions. I can intentionally choose to change my perception and select the elements in the event that I can daydream about in a positive way and when that is not possible, I will even choose thoughts that are not related to what is going on at that moment. There is nothing that matters more than the way I feel.

My life is meant to be enjoyable, fun, inspirational and meaningful. I can do, be or have everything I want, The Law of Attraction will make sure that what I desire and I do not contradict with thoughts or behaviors will become my reality. The moment I begin to shift my perception, I will begin to see the results quickly, but I will not look for the results. I will not focus on those things, which are not happening, even when I have prayed and desired for them for a long time. The more attention I pay to the absence of something, the more I push it away. I will instead just choose to feel good and then trust. I will let the universe do what it does. The universe knows what I want and everything I have ever desired, even when I don't even remember what those things were, the universe needs no reminder. I will not sabotage my wellbeing by getting frustrated over the absence of something I desire. I will not feel impatient or desperate for something to happen. I will simply acknowledge that there is a broader intelligence within and without, which is taking care of me and I must only relax and enjoy this moment and just allow things to happen when they will.

CHAPTER 3

"Expectation"

For a long time I had misinterpreted the meaning of the word expectation. I believed expectation was something I wanted to happen but it was possible that it could very well not happen. In other words, I left expectation open to different possible outcomes that were not necessarily what I had planned for. It was sort of a word I used in ways such as, "I expect to finish writing this book in a month" but I was not disappointed if it did not get done since I figured it would get done at some other time, therefore I did not give much importance to what the word really implied in a universe where all is possible.

Expectation as far as the Law of Attraction is concerned is more than a desire; it is a belief in an outcome that will come to be because I know it will. It is important in the context of this book for when I expect something and I believe and feel with strong emotion that the outcome I desire in any particular situation will be, and then it must.

I expect that I am going to be well, I expect that my desires will come true, I expect that the deal will be closed to my satisfaction, I expect to arrive safe at my destination. All of these statements and many others that may apply to any given situation are statements of certainty. The universe and my inner being are listening and eagerly paying attention to what I say, think and especially paying attention to how I feel about what I say and think about all of the time and they are gathering all of the components necessary to make this assertions a reality. I need not doubt that it will be, for if there is doubt and hesitation in my intention the universe will know and there is no fooling the universe. The universe responds to every wish and desire that I have, to every thought and intention. My guidance system lets me know the minute I want something if it should deliver or not. My vibrations and not my words are what matters to a universe that exists only as vibration. The universe knows the intention behind the words.

It is easy to know then if my desire will be fulfilled by the way I feel. If I feel doubt or I have any negative thoughts, my inner being is telling me that I am not in sync with it and therefore I need to find a way to find alignment for my desire to come true. This is nothing to be concerned about, on the contrary, because of this I now know what to do as opposed to just saying, I really desire to be well but I am not sure if it will happen, I guess I will just have to wait and see.

As I said before, I have come into this lifetime experience for a reason and that reason is to enjoy myself and to be happy. I have also come with a purpose and I am continuously fulfilling that purpose, more over, I have come equipped with my own guidance system that is aligned with the universe to help me achieve that which I desire. Soul, that spiritual, internal part of me is my connection to all that is and it wants nothing but the best for me, all that is needed is trust and belief that it is so.

This brings me now to faith, another word that feels heavy for most people. I so want to experience, see, feel, touch and smell everything. To take something just on faith feels like church is back in the picture, but that's just because the word is mostly associated with religion. Faith is the one thing that some religious people have that works, and the reason it works for them is because when I pray, with strong emotion and good intentions, when I pray with appreciation and good thoughts,

I am actually putting down all resistance in that moment. The luggage that I spoke about earlier for at least a few moments has been put down and I am now letting go. The phrases "Let go, Let God" or "What you resist, persists" is just that, no matter what the words are it all comes down to trusting, and trusting is a positive emotion and so is faith, and so is hope, all of them to different degrees.

When I let go of resistance, and resistance is but those negative thoughts, those anxious feelings, those painful emotions, whatever I want to call all that which feels bad, then I feel a sense of relief. In that moment I am not pushing against anything, if only for a moment, just like concentrating on your breathing, I have stopped the momentum of pain, sorrow, fear, loneliness and so on and I am trusting something that is wanted or desired to happen. Provided that I do not contradict my expectations after I have offered my prayers, the wishes will become a reality, because the universe does not care if I call it God, Jesus, or any other name, the universe is answering to my feeling, my emotion and my intention and that is why I can expect with certainty.

I am not asking anyone to pray or not to pray. When I ask myself to have faith I do not expect to do that successfully at first for why would it work now if it did not work in the past? I did much praying for many years. At the age of sixteen, I was kneeling all by myself in a church in Costa Rica reciting the rosary daily. I kneeled daily before a wooden Christ, lit a candle and prayed. As soon as I felt the fear that an earthquake produced in me, the praying when right out the window and was replaced with resentment and guilt. I asked myself, how could I feel this fear when I have been praying and praying all these years? God must be busy with others I thought since he is not answering me. I now know that my beliefs were flawed. Today I have faith, and that only means that I expect things to go well, I expect there is much good that will come my way and I expect that everyday I will get better and better at reducing my resistance because I also know there will be times when I will not be at my best. There will be times when situations, people or circumstances will trigger reactions that were learned and practiced for many years prior to my gaining the knowledge that all is well and things are always working out for me. I expect that when those things do come, I will take refuge in my inner being that is always well, that always loves me and that knows what is best for me. So I will go easy on myself and with such faith that I will be able to face any situation. I expect more and more to be the creator of my circumstances and less and less to have to face situations that come as a consequence of former negative thought patterns.

I think back at times when things happened which I called lucky shots or coincidences and I know that I was the creator of those events, knowing or unknowingly I had prearranged my present environment. Would it not be nice if from now on I created those moments intentionally? Well, I can, the trick is to desire something small at first, something that I can believe in, trust and have faith in. It makes no sense to wish for something that I believe cannot happen for when I believe it cannot happen, it will not.

I will become still and breathe, I will close my eyes and think no thing, after a few minutes or so, I will ask myself, what would I like? I will pay attention to what comes to mind, once I feel the desire, I will focus on that. I will see it with my mind's eye, I will stay with the thought, I will imagine I have what I desire. I will imagine how good it feels to have it, I will spend a few minutes building a good story around this thought, I will feel, really feel in my body the whole process. I will enjoy it as much as I can for as long as it feels good and then I will tell myself, I expect this to be! I will say it with conviction, I will trust that it is going to be as I wish it to be and I will then let the thought go. I will then continue on with my day and give no more thought to it for the rest of the day or any day after that. The universe knows everything in every moment so I need not to remind it once I have done this process. The key now is not to dwell on this desire once I let it go. I will not look for evidence of it for the more I put my attention on the absence of my desire the more I push it away. When I am able to do this, I will be amazed at what will unfold, so I will let it be.

CHAPTER

4

"I am"

I am the sum of lives lived, past and current, a constant evolution with no end for I am an eternal being. I recently saw a quote that read, "You don't have a soul, you are a soul, you have a body", another one read, "Soul … the guiding force behind our individual lives" I must have noticed these because of my belief that I am Soul and it is the larger and wiser part of me, projected into human form for the purpose of my own evolution and the evolution of all that is.

I am, and I believe that so is everyone else, a wonderful being in my essence. Soul is but a beautiful energy that when the human part of me allows the alignment between Soul and myself, which we were meant to have, my perception of life will no longer be distorted. This amazing life, that when allowed to be seen through the eyes of the universal intelligence within, then nothing is ever a problem, everything flows with grace, a universal twirling of energies develops before my eyes and I willingly surrender to the blissful joy of being.

I have always been drawn to teachings that seemed to reveal what an "enlightened" life is supposed to be like. First, as a young man and perhaps into my teen years, I was in awe of those beings that stories spoke of. Those beings that seemed to possess an inner peace I craved so much for. Growing up, when asked what I most wanted to become, I would always said I wanted to be a saint. I did not really mean I wanted to be canonized of course but I knew inside of me that what I really wanted was to feel the peace within they appeared to have. That peace that allowed them to live at ease, minds that had been able to stop all suffering and could now be of great service to others. I felt that one who possesses this inner peace could never walk in fear. I believed they allowed Soul to guide them throughout their lives.

I was in equal awe of Buddhist monks, as I perceived them to also have this inner peace. Just looking at one seemed to inspire safety, calmness and a sense of fulfillment, and I wanted that for me more than anything else. It was because of this strong desire that the universe has found the way to bring it to me now. I was shown this path many of times, but my stubborn beliefs would keep it from arriving and so the saying, "What you resist, persists", was a mantra I continued to allow to keep me away from my desires.

The wisdom of these so called "enlightened" beings, those who are living and those who came before, most likely came to them at the point of realizing the connection they as Souls had with the universe. They realized that a quiet mind could see beyond the ordinary, they had learned to be the masters of thought and not its slaves.

I was enslaved to thought as many are. I thought that if I was given a brain to think, then thinking must be what I should do. There is no question that thinking is a wonderful gift that when used in a positive way can create unimaginable wonders, however, when enslaved to negative thoughts, the creations are also unimaginable, the monstrosities I would allow were just as great. I am, is the essence of life. Being is that which allows all to happen, and if I am to learn anything, it is not to pollute my being with thoughts that contradict those beliefs.

I am, is what I am. The addition of labels that may follow the statement "I am" is wherein lies the distortion. "I am a writer" may sound simple enough and it serves a purpose in perhaps a conversation I may be engaged in for the purpose of communication, but the truth is that I am not a writer, I am a being who writes, and writing is a medium that I use to give expression to the being within and not a title that may lead to unwanted interpretations. When identifying with things, there is a risk of loss, so it is best to first connect with Soul where attachment cannot be for Soul enjoys all but owns nothing and when I own no thing, there is no loss. I connect with Soul when I quiet my mind and when the feeling I am experiencing is a positive one. In that state I can then just be the "I am" I was meant to be.

Many believe that detachment from all things physical is the spiritual way and therefore believe that riding themselves of all materiality is the "enlightened" way, the only way towards the feeling of peace within. I, however, feel not such thing. Enjoying all that life has to offer is to appreciate the evolution we have all created throughout time and I will not allow the negative opinions of others to spoil the enjoyment of all that is, and that includes material things.

My purpose in life is to create, to enjoy and most of all, to be, and in being I can make use of all that exists and enjoy all I desire. I choose not to live by others example but rather by making use of my own guidance system for I am unique, and even though the examples and teachings of others may be useful, even inspiring and much appreciated, it is my knowing which creates the most satisfaction at a personal level that no other can experience but me. Having things, going places and enjoying whatever it is that I like is just using that which is available to me at any given time. I own nothing, in fact no one owns anything, I am merely borrowing, using, playing with, and enjoying whatever it may be until I make the transition to the non-physical, as they say, "You take nothing with you when you die." There is no benefit to anyone when I sacrifice and suffer, and why should I do that to myself? I certainly do not wish it upon others. I am; I am love, I am appreciative, I am thankful, I am joy, I am giving, I am compassionate, I am worthy, I am happy. That is life and thoughts can get me to this things or it can keep me from them.

I chose to live, not by the guidance of others, even though I will appreciate their contributions. I will choose not to read those things that may plant negativity in me, I will choose not to hear that which will provoke negative emotions in me, I will chose not to be where being present feels negative to me and or others, I will chose to be selective about people, places and things that may in any ways disrupt the flow of my being. I wish nothing but wellness unto others but must importantly I wish it most, unto myself.

I cannot avoid all situations and experiences that present themselves in my experience that may feel negative and that is not my intent. However, it is my intention to not allow thoughts about any situation distract me from my purpose. I also know that there will be times when I will not succeed and therefore I will feel negative emotions. I will then intend to be fine with it, I will want it to be a learning experience, because all situations are but I will exercise control and I will monitor my thoughts, so that I will not be derailed for long. I also know that I will always know when thoughts are in charge for I will feel either good or I will not and as I mentioned before, this is how Soul lets me know where I am and how I am doing at all times.

There are many theories on how to live life, many of methods that people have found to be "the way". Their ways are not necessarily my own, unless I find them to resonate with me and therefore I may implement them into my life for my own benefit.

I have listened to audiobooks, I have listened to speeches and lectures and there are advertisements and all kinds of things trying to sell me, sort of speak, their ways on how to live life. Religions wanting to impose their beliefs on me, so many to choose from it is hard to grasp and fully understand even one of them. There are teachings whose intents are to help me choose a better way of life; meditation, healthy eating, exercise, this diet or that other one, vitamins and supplements are encouraged as well. It may feel at times overwhelming to pick what is right for me. I can go crazy trying to figure out which way to go. The fact that all this information exists, speaks to the desire of man to become more, to feel better. There are some exceptions of course, but most of what is out there for me to consider, even when I determine is of no relevance for me, it has been of help to others who have implemented the methods given with much success.

The key for me is not to become overwhelmed in the moments I feel stressed over which route to take, if thoughts such as, "Why am I not doing this, when I know it would be good for me?", "Why am I not consistent?", "What if I forget this or that?". All of these thoughts would be more hindrance than help when trying to achieve wellbeing for wellbeing is my natural state of being and it only gets negatively affected when negative thoughts get in the way. Soul knows only wellbeing. The universe is wellbeing and it is in the not recognizing and allowing this wellbeing to flow through me that things get out of balance. Soul wants nothing but good for me, all I need to do is to ease up, go easy on myself and relax. All I really need is to allow myself to just be.

To be in harmony with the universe is to be the "I am" that I am and for that to be I must care about how I feel, it is that simple. I will care about me and me first, for when I am well, not only I benefit but everything and everyone around me benefits as well. It is when I am well, when I am happy and joyful, that my interaction with others is happy and joyful too. By caring about me, I am also caring about others in an even more powerful way. No one benefits from my unhappiness, so in my being selfish I am in fact being selfless.

To take care of myself I will choose first to monitor my thoughts and practice no negativity at all, especially when practicing meditation or any other positive method of alignment. I will allow myself to be present and feel Soul within, which is the source of all that is good. I want to ask myself at all times, "What would I like to do now?", "What would feel good right now?". In times of silence and in times of quietude, the desire for a good experience will appear and the moments of inspiration will come. I will know my next step when I allow all to be as it is at this moment, when I ask for nothing and I think no thought and I just perceive and sense everything around me without projecting any thoughts. As I take some time to see, touch and smell whatever is pleasant at any moment, I am allowing life to happen, I am allowing myself to be. When I let go of worries and fears and allow the moment, this moment, to be and I allow myself to be part of this moment without judgment or commentaries, I am allowing life to happen. I allow things to be and in my desire to enjoy this moment, time stops and life is the way I always want it to be.

There is much beauty in being and seeing the manifestation of positive events unfold in my life when I am not expecting, yes, not expecting anything to be or happen can also be a source of joy. This is a different kind of expectation than the one I referred to in the previous chapter as the absolute knowing that something you desire will happen. It is the coming to fruition of a previous expectation that even though you knew would happen, you did not know when or how it would manifest and as they say, "Things happen when you least expect it." and there it is. In this one moment of just being, when I am not waiting for that which I want to happen to appear, in that perfect moment of simply allowing life to unfold, my desired is revealed.

CHAPTER 5

"Mental Illness"

Early in my life I felt I was different. I felt something, I sensed I was unique, just to find out later on that what I was feeling was something that was probably part of growing up and that everyone else was most likely feeling the same way.

I was bullied at school and being that I was an A+ student I was picked on quite a bit. If this was the beginning of my lifelong struggle with depression I do not know. I was constantly overwhelmed by fear, insecurity and feelings of guilt in my teenage years and beyond. I refused to take any kind of medications for a long time until I decided in my early twenties that I had no other choice. This decision put me on a long road of therapies and a myriad of antidepressants that were prescribed in many different dosages. I believed they did lessen my symptoms for a while, until a new medication would come onto the market and from that one to the next one, it went on and on. The best the medications were able to do, was to keep me functioning in society. Depression, fear, worry and anxiety remained, but for the most part the situation was manageable. For some reason I thought that I would eventually overcome this illness and would find a way to be well and therefore no longer have the need for any medication.

As it turns out, this did not go as I thought. As I got older I developed stronger symptoms of depression, anxiety, compulsive behaviors, phobias, paranoia and even some panic attacks. Late into my forties I was doing so poorly I sought professional help once again after many years of just dealing with it through my regular doctor. This time I was diagnosed with bipolar depression and was therefore taken off the antidepressants and prescribed different types of medications to fight this new discovery.

I realized at that time that not only was I not going to rid myself of the lifelong depression but that now I had a mental illness for which there was no cure, so I fell into an even deeper sense of despair and sadness. I felt doomed. Three years of treatment as a bipolar patient and two more psychologists confirming the diagnosis I was worse than I ever was before. The new medications I was taking to deal with this illness were disturbing my brain in ways I had not experienced before, to the point that I was not functioning at all and was seriously thinking that death was near. I could see how others in my situation would have opted to commit suicide as their only alternative. When you find yourself in a place so dark that life makes no sense whatsoever and you loathe your existence, this feels like the next likely outcome. However, even though thoughts about suicide had entered my mind twice in my life, I always felt a glimmer of hope. I somehow would remember the teachings like this well known saying, "This too will pass" and understood that nothing ever stays the same for long. For me however, "long" did not apply for I had been in pain for what felt like eternity. I held on and continued my quest with whatever energy I could muster and I looked for guidance. I would cling to anything that could help or even showed the possibility of being helpful.

I speak of my experience with mental illness so that the reader understands that suffering does not have to be endless even if it appears that way at any given time. I know that when one feels hopeless, it seems there is nothing anyone can tell you that will help and those who attempt to help, even with the best of intentions, only succeed in making you feel worse. I know that for me, being left alone was all I wanted even when inside I was screaming out for help. I believed that the help I could seek out on my own was the most helpful. I found comfort in listening to spiritual and motivational audiobooks and those in fact were the most help I received. The wisdom I found in some of them resonated with me somehow. To make a long story short, after three years I made the decision to stop the medications I was taking and I went back on the antidepressants. This turned out to be a good decision for it helped me get out of the abyss and I was able to avoid the dreaded idea of Electroconvulsive Therapy that by then was the only option left and was strongly advised by three different experts.

Once I became functional and was feeling better, I stumbled upon alternative medicine. The idea had been mentioned to me before by some acquaintances but at the time I had no idea how to go about it so I did not give it much thought. This time however, I decided to give it a try. This turned out to be perfect for me at the time and I followed the new protocol with great results. I was feeling better than I had ever felt before; acupuncture, herbal medicines and a daily coffee enema did wonders for me.

I then became more and more interested in listening to as much information I could find online. I was eager to feel even better, my desire to be more spiritual was growing and it took me somehow of all place to YouTube, where I listened to lectures, interviews, and audiobooks. I just could not get enough. I found more and more things to listen to every day, spending countless hours saturating my brain with knowledge and wisdom that I had not heard before that felt so good to me I had to try it for myself.

It was this research I was now enthralled in where I found the information I was looking for all of these years and once I heard it, I understood it, I believed in it and I practiced it, that I was able to feel well and I felt I would be able to no longer have the need for any type of medication, alternative or pharmaceutical. I had finally found the "secret" of life and in it. I found peace, the feeling of peace I searched for all my life was now here and it felt real, it felt clear, it felt so simple and so logical that it inspired me to write this book. It is so much my true desire that my words and the words of others that may flow through me in this writing will touch and change your life for the better.

Mental illnesses such as depression and anxiety are only chemical imbalances because of our perceptions, our interpretations of events and circumstances. Those are the reason we suffer this afflictions. I say this with no hesitation, but I do understand that if you are in such negative states of mind as depression and anxiety for example, you will find this to be absurd, but since I have been in your shoes, I hope that fact alone will give you hope.

A chemical imbalance implies that there is something wrong with our brains. If I were to call it a chemical or a cellular reaction to the way I feel, I believe it would be more accurate. A totally "normal" person has chemical imbalances all the time, let's say for example I am a "normal" person and I hear the doorbell ring. I open the door and I see people holding balloons and one of these people has a huge mockup check for ten million dollars. I, who just minutes ago was sitting in my kitchen having some cereal, not thinking about much of anything would be in shock. In a matter of seconds an instant chemical change in my brain manifests as feelings of excitement and joy. Chemicals in my brain, in fact my entire body change all the time. I can just go and look in the mirror and see the physical face looking back at me is nothing like the person that was there twenty years ago. But I am the same; it feels no different to look in the mirror now as compared to twenty years ago. The way I think very much affects the balance or imbalance at any given time so the importance of caring about my thoughts is as important for my brain health as it is for my whole body. As I take care of my thoughts, I take care of all that happens to me from head to toes.

The thoughts that I think create my world and that includes my body and my brain. The chemical imbalance anywhere in my body can be adjusted through my thought process, not medications. I do not suggest stopping any medications now and telling myself that I am well and that is all for that would probably not turn out well at all. Stopping any kind of medication without the supervision of a doctor can be very detrimental to one's health. A gradual change in my habitual thinking pattern is the best approach. I know how I feel and what to do next, it is a process that will amaze, and it sure did me.

I have faith that I will be depressed tomorrow if I am feeling depressed today, so why not have faith that I can get better?

And in doing so, I will. I have faith that I will be broke tomorrow if I have no money today, so why not have faith on things getting better? I have faith that I am going to be ill tomorrow because I am ill today, why not have faith that my health will improve? Faith is but a belief in something I do not yet know exists, so the fact I have a belief of tomorrow being a certain way is also based on faith because I do not know what will happen a half hour from now. Tomorrow is an illusion, a projection of the mind, a fantasy I have convince myself to be true.

While it is probably not likely that I will come out of a strong emotion such as depression or despair by sheer will power since I cannot stop the momentum suddenly after months or years of suffering, I can definitely improve the way I feel by doing some simple things. Just taking small steps at a time, so I want to get myself to feeling hopeful first. I can achieve this by beginning to pay attention to my breathing, and this will stop my mind from creating any thoughts.

I have hundreds if not thousands of thoughts on any given day, they are probably the same or similar thoughts to the ones I had the day before, a habitual pattern I have learned over time. I know I can only think one thought at a time. Even when it appears that I am having many thoughts at once, this is not so, it only appears that way because I move from one thought to the next so rapidly that it is hard to notice the change. Knowing this may be comforting for then I can start guiding my thoughts in the direction I need them to go.

Again, I will concentrate on my breathing. Concentrating on my breathing may be difficult at first, thoughts will try to intrude many times while I am involved in this process, but if I just allow the thoughts to be and consciously acknowledge that the thoughts are there and I consciously chose to go back to my breathing without judgment, without criticizing or blaming myself for not being able to concentrate, then I will start to improve. I will breathe in and breathe out, I will follow the air that goes in and out of my nose and I will notice my abdomen expanding and contracting. I will let go of all thoughts that want to take over, I will just simply tell them, not now, I am counting my breaths and you need to wait. I will practice this until I have mastered it.

Some people will not have much trouble doing this, if this is the case, then that is great. Some people may find that being out in nature makes them feel better, some will find relief in going to sleep for a while or taking a walk. If I can identify something that I can do that will feel better than what I am doing at this moment, I will do that. Nothing matters more than improving how I feel at this moment.

Visualizing is another really helpful method to use. I have all kinds of movies going on in my head sometimes that I cannot seem to be able to stop, so how about changing the film? I will visualize my own movie, I will create a scenario that is pleasing, I will see myself on the beach, mountain, on a boat fishing, anywhere that I think would be a nice place to be and I will then create a really good movie. I will not allow my mind to wander off and try to trick me into going back to the bad movie I was playing by saying things like, this is not real; I know reality to be different. This is just an exercise; a game that I choose to play because I know it will make me feel better. I will write it down, I will write the script on paper if possible, for by writing down my fantasy it will be even more effective. I will remind myself I am doing this because I want to stop the madness, so I will stay in the moment and I will allow myself sometime for me to get away from misery.

I will tell myself, this too will pass, nothing stays the same for long, I do not know what is going to happen but I believe it will be good. I am going to apply these thoughts because I want to feel better and I will do whatever it takes to accomplish that. The truth is that I create my own life even if I do not believe I do. I can do it consciously or I can do it unconsciously. I look at the thoughts I have and I see that the despair has been ongoing and that is because I only attract that which I offer so if I am sad and feeling down on myself I am perpetuating the conditions that will show up in my experience over and over again. The movie I have created has evolved into an epic film with many sequels.

Conditions cannot change until I give myself the opportunity to start thinking thoughts that are different than the ones I have been thinking. Even if it sounds impossible to change because my current way of thinking is engraved deep in my mind, I know deep within that I can change them. I will ask only that I try and that will show me the proof and I will then feel encouraged and I will begin feeling better and better. This is so important that I feel I must summarize and reaffirm this process.

I concentrate on my breathing, I do not judge, blame or feel bad for not being able to do it. I will just keep trying as long as it feels that I can do it. I will not get frustrated for this will just make things worse and confirm my negative believes. I will fantasize! I will create my make-believe world, I will give myself permission to create an alternative reality for a little while and once I find some comfort in this process I will continue the practice it in subsequent days. I will remind myself I have practiced the way I am for many years, so giving myself a month or two is nothing in comparison. It is my intent to believe the movie I create, I will feel the emotions as I think or write down the content of my film, and I will make it a comedy if possible. I believe that just trying these two things alone will give me great relief from the negative life I have been living.

Once I start to feel better, I will take times during the day, as many times as possible to monitor my thoughts, I will remember that my inner being is here with me, I will acknowledge the presence of me and I and say thank you, source energy will let me know by the way I feel if the thoughts I am having need to change or not. Whenever I perceive the presence of negative thoughts, I will challenge them, I will strive to find a reason why the thought is wrong and my inner being and I are right. I will try to switch my focus from the negative thoughts to something else. I do not have to pretend and say to myself I am happy when I am feeling sad, that is not what I am doing here. What I do want is to shift my attention even if slightly to a better place. Pretending I do not feel the way I am feeling right now is not the solution, the idea is just to move away from that place to one that feels better.

For example, let's say I am feeling really sad thinking that nobody cares about me and I feel lonely. I will catch these thoughts and emotions and bring my conscious awareness to them and then I will stop them from evolving. I will acknowledge how I feel, I will then do some breathing exercises, I will take a moment and then I will challenge the thoughts, I will tell myself that those thoughts are not probably true or perhaps a bit exaggerated because I know that my mother loves me very much and also, I think I probably do care about me since I am reading this book, I must care even if a little bit if I am looking for relief. The idea is to move myself away from the unpleasant experience and into a better feeling place gradually, I want to go slow and steady for I will have a better chance of success that way.

It sounds simple and silly perhaps but taking these baby steps are crucial to breaking the habitual patterns and the more I do this and the more I find positive things in my life to feel appreciative of, no matter how small they are, the quicker my life will turn around. Before I know it, I will be feeling like I have never felt before.

Some may say that all of this sounds simple and easy but the reality is that I feel miserable and that is just the way it is. I know, I felt exactly that way too, but I followed these steps little by little, I had nothing to lose, anything would have been a gain for me, no matter how small the shift.

What I can tell you now though is, that reality is not what is happening right now but my interpretation of the conditions as I perceive them in this present moment. The moment I begin to ponder the possibility that my interpretation may be flawed, I begin to give myself a chance for change. Things are not as they appear to be unless I unwillingly make them appear.

CHAPTER 6

"Placebo"

There is a strong correlation between thought and wellbeing, not only mental health but the entire body as well. The mind and body connection is undeniable, thought is so powerful that often, the moment I have a thought I feel the reaction to that thought in my body almost immediately. For example, the feeling of nausea produced when I experience a certain smell in the air. There is even the sensation of nausea in reaction to certain thoughts and that is your body letting you know that your thoughts are not in alignment with Soul. I personally feel tightness in my stomach when I feel tense. This is my inner being letting me know that I am having a reaction to negative thoughts.

There are many accounts of people having spontaneous healing. There are many cases in which science could not explain how the full recovery of an individual who was ill occurred and how it was possible that the complete absence of illness was permanent.

Medical trials are a testimony to the power of thought in relation to the health of a person. People are selected and divided into two groups where one group is given the trial medication and the other group a placebo or sugar pill. At the end of the trial some of the subjects who were given the non-pharmaceutical medication or placebo, experienced the same or even greater improvement in their conditions than those who where administered the actual medication.

There is a story that I heard not long ago that illustrates the power of the placebo effect very clearly. The story goes as follows. Once, in ancient times, masses of people would travel long distances just to be able to touch the old dried up bones that were believed to belong to an ancient being who possessed healing powers, these believers were said to touched these bones and received instant healing, a complete disappearance of their illnesses. One day, some thieves stole the sacred bones and the caretakers of these bones found themselves not knowing what to do and scrambling to find a solution quickly since there were many people coming from far away lands expecting to be healed. The caretakers decided to take the bones of a dead man who in life had been a murderer and used them to replace the blessed bones. The story goes on to say that the believers continued to be healed even after touching the sinner's bones.

This is a great testament to the power of the mind and the power of thought. Faith, the belief in taking a pill or touching some bones is such that the healing occurs. It is that which I think and believe with powerful strong feeling, that determines the duration or even the cure of my illness and suffering.

The natural way of the body is to be healthy. I believe that I intended to come into this world with perfect health. Illness creeps in through thought, I unknowingly used thought and behavior in ways that disagreed with the knowing of Soul and the universe which as I mentioned before know only of wellbeing. The thoughts I have in any situation, if perceived negatively cause the imbalance of the cells in my body. I have attracted conditions based on my interpretation of experiences and subsequent reactions to them.

I say unknowingly because I would not consciously choose to be sick, I always want to feel I have perfect health. In the same way that my pattern of thoughts and behaviors influence the life I will live, illness shows up the same way. My thoughts, perceptions and interpretations on whatever subject or experience I am having at this moment, determine the path I have chosen.

When I find myself in a state of anxiety or depression, when I find that my current experience is stressful in any way, this interpretation of my current situation will bring about all kinds of negative outcomes, one of which includes disease in my body. At the same time, once I acknowledge this is what is happening and I begin to take steps in the direction of thinking differently and I do not to let my habitual negative patterns take the reins of my life, I can start to see the improvement and wellbeing will manifest.

The idea that you can cure yourself without medication sounds farfetched and illogical to many. I am so accustomed to receiving medical treatment for all kinds of diseases and illnesses that I may not even think about a more natural approach. It seems I will only seek alternative medicine or alternative treatments when I have exhausted all possible medical treatment options. There is great value in modern medicine and I believe that science has come a long way. However, modern medicine for the most part only treats the illness and not the cause of it and in doing so, it fails to fully benefit humanity. If I can eradicate the source of any disease by eliminating its cause, I would not need to treat it for it would not exist.

There are cases in modern medicine where the eradication of a disease has been achieved. Polio is a good example, but I would encourage myself to seek out a more natural approach first or even simultaneously use both approaches in some cases as opposed to waiting and using it as a last resort. I will strongly encourage myself to think and behave in a more positive way before and or after a disease has manifested since the cause of the disease may very well have been cause by an established old negative pattern.

In my experience, I can say with certainty that all illnesses and diseases that came my way at one time or another were in direct correlation with my habitual, negative thought pattern. I did not realized at the time that my thoughts, and when I say thoughts I am referring to my perception and interpretation of events in my life were the culprits, along with behaviors that went hand in hand with those thoughts.

I have seen the manifestation of my thoughts into depression and anxiety and even other less serious diseases in my body. I now find, with much amazement and appreciation for the knowledge I have received that I no longer have to suffer. I have found that I can think myself away from sickness and into good health, a simple assertion such as, "not for me", becomes a powerful shield against things unwanted. Allow me to explain this process further.

I create my reality through my perception and the subsequent interpretation thereafter, to be followed by a manifestation that matches the vibration I am offering at any given time, or better said, in this moment, right now. Since nothing happens but in this moment, it is what is happening in this one experience I am having right now that determines what is to come in a future present moment.

Let's say there is a random situation happening in this one moment and I experience an emotion, and let's just say I interpret this emotion to be a funny event since I happen to be watching a film and it is a comedy. These thoughts, perceptions or interpretations happen automatically, I do not have to analyze it much for it is a pleasant experience, therefore I want to welcome it and enjoy it as much as I can. My brain does not only enjoy this feeling of wellbeing but all the cells in my body are now in harmony with my thoughts and there is a great chance now for improved health. If on the other hand I am feeling sick, it is my intention to experience none of it and since I know that joy is a great healer and sickness cannot be for long in its presence I will strive to find a way to feel happy and joyful by guiding my thoughts towards these vibrations. This is the best recipe for achieving optimal health.

I know this state of mind will not last forever since life is ever changing but I will do my best to try and achieve moments such as these more and more often. I will remind myself that I am the creator of my life and I have complete freedom to choose the thoughts that will make me feel better and better, because feeling good will not only make this one moment a success but it will also create my future success as well.

I am but the thoughts I think. I am that which my thoughts interpret, not only in my brain but the feeling expands to include all of me from head to toes. The more I think that which makes me feel good, the healthier I will be in mind and body.

Because of The Law of Attraction that runs this universe, I attract to me that which is similar to whatever I have strong feelings about, so I want to be very careful in selecting thoughts that make me feel good for I will attract goodness in doing so. By the same token, if I allow my thoughts to run wild and I let them slip into old negative patterns, the circumstances will change and I will receive negative results now and in the future as long as I continue to feel this way. The Law of Attraction will bring me more things that are a match to whatever I am feeling no matter what the experience is.

If I at this moment am having health problems and my thoughts are mostly about the problem and how bad it feels to be sick, the likelihood of getting better is diminished because my attention is on the illness or bad situation and not on the solution or the intention to feel better. If instead, I try to distract myself from this unpleasant condition and steer my thoughts in a more positive way, there is a much better chance for improvement.

I know how difficult it is to try and control my thoughts when I find myself in less than favorable circumstances. The years of negativity will creep in for sure and it will take much conscious attention to change that. But if I just lessen the blow by distracting myself or at least keep myself from dwelling over the situation, I will accomplish much better results.

My mind controls my physical body in ways I never knew it could, so whenever I find myself feeling ill, I will use my thoughts to create a different picture. I will try and imagine what it would feel like to be well, I will imagine how it would feel like to be in perfect health, I will fantasize about feeling great, I will take the time to write it down. This is the time to start a new movie and in this movie, I will be healthy and running on the beach and I will be playing with my dogs. In this movie, I will imagine I have taken the new medication and not the placebo. I will make a movie where I am the one touching the sacred bones and I have become completely healed and I will enjoy the feeling I get from the fantasy I create, but mostly I will try my best to not create any negative thoughts and feelings in the presence of pain and pay no mind to a label I have been given by a doctor. I will tell myself that I am well here and now. In the event that this movie feels like a contradiction from the way I feel as my current reality, I will tell myself that help is on the way and that things are going to get better, and little by little I will have my healthy body back. There is no contradiction in having hope, there is no contradiction in having faith and there is no contradiction in thinking that I can very well be one of those people who have experienced spontaneous healing or one of the many who refused to accept their negative conditions as permanent.

I want to always remind myself that every moment is an opportunity. If I am feeling bad right now and I begin to believe that more of the same is in store for me, I will not worry nor will I beat myself up over it. I know there will be a moment right after this one, and one after that one, when I can then change my thoughts to a more positive outlook and I will maintain that feeling and soon, before I know it, I will attract wellness instead. Every single moment is a new opportunity to improve my life. I will refuse to believe that I only get one chance in life because I know that in every single moment there is a chance.

CHAPTER 7

"Time"

Much has been written about the unconscious and subconscious mind and the ego. It is not my intent to add much on these subjects, since I find that the theories regarding them are at best very confusing and I believe they do not add much to the understanding nor are they of great benefit to my present experience. I can analyze endlessly all of these theories and become quite frustrated. I on the other hand feel that consciousness is what I am and therefore the most important thing I can focus on and consciousness happens in time, more accurately, it happens in this time, this moment, right here and right now.

Time can be a very destructive. Past, present and future are moments in time that can be help or hindrance depending on how they are perceived. It has been said that time is an illusion or even a matter of perception and on that, I am in complete agreement.

Life happens in the present moment, right here and right now. This is probably the most important piece of knowledge ever realized and for many centuries very wise men have tried to teach and help others understand the reasoning behind this concept. It is a concept that even organized religions have not misinterpreted, diluted nor deleted from their books. Perhaps because they did not see the power of this knowledge or they may have possibly assumed that man would not be able to grasp and apply it, for it seems to be one of, if not the most important teaching of all time. So important in deed that it is the single most difficult thing one can achieve consistently.

Much of man's suffering and shortcomings are caused by his inability to live in the present moment. I know it has been so in my experience and I have yet to encounter anyone with such power yet. I do feel it is absolutely crucial for a consistent state of wellbeing.

I remember listening to a book on this subject and feeling I was in the presence of sublime wisdom. It seemed to me at the time I had known this information all along and that if I could finally live by the teachings of this powerful book titled "The Power Of Now" by Eckhart Tolle, all my problems would disappear and I would finally have peace. I believed in it so much I would listen to it over and over again. I wanted to memorize this book so I could consciously apply it in my life and finally free myself of all afflictions.

So many quotes exist from wonderful thinkers, teachers and philosophers throughout history, and they all speak of the present moment, the here, the now and being present as the only way to live the "enlightened" life.

There is much suffering in time. Time overwhelmed me for very long, the past or rather thoughts about the past brought me guilt; sadness and depression just to name a few. Thoughts about the future brought me fear; stress and anxiety just to name a few as well. The present was intolerable because thoughts about past and future would keep me trapped in miserable experiences one after another. I later learned that this misery could be avoided by acknowledging that nothing ever happened in the past and nothing will ever happen in the future. I learned that everything happens in this one moment.

The past is but events, people and situations that I have access to through memory. When the past occurred, it did so in a former present moment and I can choose to allow those memories to be or not to be in my present experience by paying attention to my thoughts. The bad or negative memories, I can decide not to accept by changing the thought as soon I feel the negativity. The good and positive memories I can enjoy and allow them to be for as long as they feel good. Discarding the bad memories and allowing the good ones is very important in achieving a state of wellbeing. I will then cherish the good memories and spend as much time there as I can, and I will try to avoid the ones that do not feel good.

The future is all about my imagination, a projection of thoughts into a time that is not yet here. It is important for me to acknowledge that the future will happen in the present moment, there is never, ever, anything happening in the future since the future does not exist. It is important for me to acknowledge that nothing ever happened in the past and nothing will ever happen in the future but everything that happens is the experience I am having right now.

This one moment is all there is, in this one moment creation happens, in this one moment I can choose to look back and feel good or bad depending on the thoughts I currently hold about any subject. In this one moment I can look forward and I can choose to feel good or bad depending on the thoughts I currently hold about any subject. I want to care about this moment more than anything else. I want to use this moment right here and right now to create my life because whatever I do in this moment will influence my future experiences. I will create long epic wonderful movies about the life I want to live. This is the perfect time to tell the universe what I want.

I do not have to accept anything undesirable. I have my will and my thoughts to help me make this moment a good experience. I must consciously bring myself into this moment so I can enjoy the life I have and the life I want to have, knowing I cannot control others but I certainly have control over my own experience. So I must be conscious of this time I have right now and make it great.

If my situation at this moment is not desirable, if I am frustrated or depressed, the very least I can do is bring awareness to my breathing, that will automatically place me in the present moment. I must worry not about what is to come for I have no control over it and worrying can only make it worse. I have only control of the way I feel, the most important thing in my life should be my awareness of this moment I am in, whatever this moment is like for me, I must take control of it and make myself feel better. If I feel OK, I will try to feel better, if I feel good, I will try to feel even better because how I feel right now determines what my next moment will feel like and then the next one and the next one after that and before I realize it, the future that I imagined will show up and I will find my creation in a moment much like this one.

My awareness of this one moment in time cannot be expressed strongly enough. I am here, right now, standing in my shoes thinking about so many things I have picked up from my past that bring me to all kinds of conclusions. It is hard to let go of all I have experienced, all that I have learned. It is so difficult to imagine my life being much different since "common sense" is telling me that it is what it is, and it is. What it is right now is, but it is because of my perception, which is making it so. My learned habits of thinking do not allow for much variation, however, realizing that what is, is the end result of a thinking pattern I have become accustomed to live by, I can take a conscious step back and analyze the situation like I would any other and question and ask myself if I want to continue living this way.

I would encourage myself to disregard all that I have been told. Things I have learned from my parents, people in my environment, what I have heard and read in books. I will assume that all of it could very possibly be not accurate. I will just take every beliefs that I have right now and question it no matter how strong I feel about them, no matter if it is something I have learned through generations, no matter if it was taught in school, no matter if it came from a source I relied on wholeheartedly. I will question everything that I do not know for sure because I have not experienced it myself and then question those that I have experienced as well for even those beliefs I have known as truths may not be so. I must question and ask myself, "Is it true because I really know it is or is it because my interpretation or perception made it so?

If I were to start today, right here, right now with a clean slate and begin to sense as opposed to interpret my experiences, I will probably find that many preconceived notions I previously held may not be the truth at all.

Throughout history there have been many famous writers, philosophers, psychologists and others that after offering theories that at the time seemed to be "the truth" and everyone adopted it as such were later discredited by others. Just believing something that seemingly appears to be true does not make it so. There have been groups of researchers who have come to different results on the same topic. I suggest there is no better guide to the truth than the one you have within. When I consciously put my attention on how I feel about anything at any particular moment and in any particular situation, I will find that the greatest wisdom comes from within.

It has been said that words do not teach, experiences do, but words do help in directing me to knowledge that I previously lacked. Words can be a source of much negativity, words can be misinterpreted and they have been misinterpreted many times. There are many words that when used incorrectly can do much damage; therefore, I would encourage myself to not get attached to any words. I will accept words only if they are helpful in guiding me towards where I want to go.

I have tried to use simple words that do not carry a great potential for misinterpretations or that may lose their meaning or intention of use. I have chosen to use words such as thing or things as to not create an undesirable mental image on the reader's mind. It is my intention to simply point you towards a path to your own knowledge within and not to force any beliefs on you. I am merely giving my opinion in all subjects with an expectation that it will resonate within you and help you in your life's journey.

CHAPTER

8

"Reincarnation"

The idea of reincarnation is accepted in many cultures, so perhaps it is not that radical of an idea even though it is not a belief shared by most of the world. I must say I personally had trouble with this concept and every time I seemed to begin to open up to the possibility of it being real someone would say something that made me think twice. It is interesting for me to notice that I now finally accept something that was shown to me at different times in my life and that I had rejected, I guess I was not ready. As they say, "When the student is ready, the teacher will appear."

I believe I am source energy as well as flesh and bones. I will call it Soul and I. We are two only at those times when I am not feeling well and not in sync with Soul. The moment I feel the connection, which is when I do feel well; we are no longer two but one and the same. Perhaps a better way to say this is that most of who I am, is a non-physical energy that flows through my physical body and it is part of a different dimension but fully present here and now. When this non-physical me is realized by me, we fuse together and my life experience becomes one of joy. Everything flows with ease, things happen in harmony and perfect alignment. Inspiration is present and the life I intended to live becomes a reality.

This source energy flows through me, in me, and all around me. This source energy or Soul has lived many physical lives and in all of these voyages the purpose has always been the same, to live an earthly experience in joy, and in every experience the intention has been to become more and to evolve. I do not know how many lifetimes I have lived and I am not at all interested in this information for it would probably not bring me to a better understanding of my experience today. I do know that every experience was important and every one of them contributed to the being I am today. This person that I am today is an evolution enhanced over each lifetime.

As I think about it, the fact that I have an affinity for something, whatever that something may be, this calling as it is sometimes called or purpose, the idea that this is what I was born to do and whenever I am told I have a natural gift, to me these are signs of a previous existence and I am here to develop these attributes further for the development and growth of my being.

There is not a God who sent me here to earth and said, "You will have this ability in this field," and it is not by chance that I was drawn to become a great chef or a music genius just because I was exposed to my mother's cooking or I took a music class which forged what my future would become. These characteristics have always been a part of me and each time I have reincarnated back into physical form I have honed those "gifts" and I have become better than I was before.

Some say, "You have an old soul." It seems to me that some people are wiser beyond their years, some appear to have the perfect surroundings, the rich parents, perfect circumstances and much "luck" while others seem to be lacking all of it. What if everyone chose those conditions and circumstances from whatever vantage point they had and actually and intentionally picked them before reincarnating in this lifetime because they knew it would offer them the opportunity for growth? What if we are all at different levels in our evolution and our journeys have landed us here in the perfect place at the perfect time?

If I just take as an example siblings who were raised the same way, had the same set of parents and the same surroundings, and they all appear to be completely different, their paths seemed to have developed parallel to each other but they turned out to not be so. One seems smarter than the others, even when the seemingly less intelligent are the ones who pursued higher education. Things seem to work out easier for some more than the others. Could it be that this is because they are all at a different stage on their journeys? The wisdom acquired in their lives, past and present are different. They have chosen different experiences, they are honing different skills, they are all a different soul that has a completely different set of desires and who covet different things.

We like to call "geniuses" those rare humans who we deem outstanding and special, either because they seem to have great intelligence or amazing skill sets that are more advanced than the rest, they seem to have been special since birth, possessing attributes and skills only granted to a very few individuals. But what if these are ancient souls who decided to embody the "genius"' body for the purpose of guiding humanity, for the purpose of showing others how wonderfully amazing life is meant to be and to be an example and inspiration for others.

Most feel purpose early in life, we identify rather quickly with the sorts of things we like and enjoy. The journey may be delayed by circumstances and the surroundings and perhaps that is why some realize their dreams late in life. Whatever the circumstances are, the desires do not disappear but at best they just stay dormant for a while. What if it was all perfectly timed and we all intended our lives to be unfolding exactly the way they are? What if we chose to come just for the experience, without a particular purpose but instead just to be here and have the experience this lifetime has to offer? The possibilities are endless.

This realization is very liberating. To think and to know that I am here now, that I was here before upon this earth at an earlier time, and that I will be back again to continue with my own development and to enjoy life and know that death is joy as well, for being non-physical, being spirit is an even more joyful and pleasant experience. This concept would rid humanity of the fear that keeps it in bondage. There is no death as perceived by most, the physical dissolution of the body is nothing but a transition between lifetimes and for some a transition to a blissful, eternal, non-physical life.

This brings me to the knowledge I have acquired that makes much sense to me now. It was the mathematics of reincarnation that really put doubt in my mind when others would explain their opposition to this idea. For me, it seemed impossible for the number of people on earth changes all the time and did not correlate with the number of people who die and the number of people alive plus the new births did not compute well in my head. I thought if there were let us say the first ten people on earth and five of them died, twenty are born, then two die and ten more are born and so on, I would then ask, where are those people coming from? Not enough have died to reincarnate again. Seeing it from this perspective, made me question the belief in reincarnation.

I now understand that this does not work that way, there is not a revolving door of recycled beings, and not all the beings that ever existed are here now or planning a come back. There are many beings that are non-physical that are not interested in the physical experience. These beings have other purposes and I believe many are so evolved that a physical experience would no longer be of any benefit to them for they have achieved the end of their physical voyage but they are still nonetheless evolving for our growth here on earth benefits the entire universe, which they are also a part of. I believe these being are very involved in life on this planet from a non-physical perspective and in many cases communicate with physical beings for the benefit of humanity.

Many have been called masters or teachers and they possess eternal knowledge, wisdom beyond what I can grasp or even comprehend in my human form. I believe they are guides that are ever present in our lives for they are universal energy not completely separate from us since we too have universal energy flowing through us. We all possess this knowledge to some degree perhaps and it is through our life experiences, this one and the ones before that we are exposed to the unlimited wisdom that exists.

Thinking of generations past, it is easy to see that man has evolved tremendously even if I only take into consideration the past one hundred years. Things that were unimaginable even just twenty years ago are a reality today. Imagination has created a world that continues to expand. Can you imagine the wonders that await us all in future lifetimes?

The way it works is simple but genius. I was born, reincarnated from the spirit world, I had experiences, the experiences automatically created evolution, I became more than I was before, I experience a physical death and reemerge into the non-physical realm taking with me the new and improve version of me. My improved version then returns to physical form and begins to evolve once again and on and on until I arrived here, where I am continuously evolving, enjoying the progress achieved through previous reincarnations and once more I am gathering knowledge and experiences that make me become more than I was. It is exciting to be here now to share with others who I have become and at some point I will depart once again but this time I will have no fear for I know this dimension of eternal energy that awaits me is a wonderful place where I can look back and rejoice, enjoy my creation and look upon the world with much appreciation, knowing I will be eager to return at some point to continue the journey. This will never end because I am eternal and I will become more and more each time.

The evolution potential of my being cannot even be imagined, but I can live today and feel empowered by the knowledge that there is purpose in all of it. Even in the smallest of things there is being, there is energy in even those things that I may interpret to be insignificant for they would not be if it were different. The plants, the animals, humanity and everything in the universe is ever changing and evolving. There is no end to the becoming.

There are many who feel that we do not choose our circumstances in this lifetime, that we could not possibly be the creators of our own lives. Why would anyone choose negative conditions and perhaps the biggest objection is, what about the innocent children? Children or babies could not have possibly chosen terrible illnesses to be part of their experiences. I have asked these questions myself, and many more. I do not pretend to have the answers but what I do have is other questions.

Since I was non-physical source energy before I entered my body and therefore I was full consciousness with universal wisdom, could it be possible that I would come into this world from non-physical and decide that I would sacrifice this one lifetime, however short it may be, for the purpose of helping others? What if I intended through my seemingly horrible experience to teach something to those around me? What if I selflessly felt the experience would mostly be just to benefit the development of others? As non-physical I knew that I would reemerge after my physical experience into the blissful place I came from. The thing that is clear for me is that I cannot possibly know nor was it my intent to identify, sort out, and find the answers for the others who inhabit this planet. I cannot possibly know the reasons why others choose to do what they do, I have plenty to consider within my own experience.

I would like to touch briefly on the subject of Karma in this chapter for it seems pertinent. Karma has become a popular word in our society, the idea that we are here on this earth to fix mistakes from previous lifetimes makes no sense to me, and how can I right wrongs I have no knowledge of making? Even in this lifetime If I see someone who does something I perceive as negative I may believe that Karma will take care of him or her somewhere down the road, but if I look at history, I can see the many atrocities that have been committed throughout where there seemed to be no punishments for the perpetrators. I did not reincarnate to right wrongs or to fix a broken world or to look at others' lives and make judgments as to what is right or wrong for them. Since we all have our own inner beings to guide us and our purposes are not the same, I will wish everyone well on their journeys and I will pay close attention to mine for if my journey is on track, we all benefit.

CHAPTER

9

"Money"

It seems like these days the word "money" stirs up all kinds of feelings in people, one of which is resentment. There seems to be a perception of income inequality in society, where the very wealthy are perceived as being greedy, unscrupulous people who care not about the rest who seem to be more impoverished by the minute. The rich are getting richer and the poor are getting poorer. Even if this belief is accurate in many instances, I believe this is certainly not the case for all. We have the most charitable society in all of history, however, charity will not bring poverty to extinction but a change in mindset could.

Regardless of how much money anyone has, that will not change my personal economic situation, for other's experiences cannot affect mine. In fact, nothing can affect my life experience unless I allow it to happen. People have total control over their own lives but none over others. Influence may be asserted but only when I allow that influence to be part of my experience. Since I create my own life and this means all aspects of my life, my wealth, my health and everything else for that matter, it is but through thought that I determine my destiny.

There are countless books on how to get rich. There are plenty of methods and even gimmicks that are used to achieve wealth. To some, making a lot of money requires a lot of hard work, others chose gambling and others may inherit the wealth. I suggest that no matter how I go about getting rich if that is my desire, the most important accomplishment must be to be content in whatever situation I may be in and the wealth and every other desirable outcome will come to be.

Many believe that success is measured in dollars, but I believe this is never the case for I know of many very wealthy dissatisfied people and success is a very satisfying experience. Success means different things to different people, a very happy person is more successful than all the unhappy billionaires alive, as the saying goes, money can't buy happiness. It also cannot buy love or good health.

To see wealth and unhappiness dwell together is a very sad thing. I often asked myself, how is it possible that someone with so much money, someone with access to anything they could desire can suffer so much? Why can't they find the guidance they need when others with so little are able to achieve peace within? And the answer comes down to one word, thought.

If I cannot find satisfaction in having a billion dollars, in having my dream home or more than one or in having any material thing I desire, it is not because money is evil and being wealthy is a course, but because what I have in the bank, I lack in my connection with Soul. There is no amount of money that will give me peace of mind as long as I struggle with negative thoughts.

There is the belief I should rid myself of all material things if I want to be a spiritual person. The belief that wealthy people are sinners is misguided. Here it is, once again the opinion of others trying to persuade the rest to live their lives by their rules. Why should I do such a thing? Is my being poor going to somehow solve the scarcity of money in others? Of course not, in the same way that I will not see my bank account grow just because I know others who are rich. On this subject, as well as all others, I am willing to listen to all and then make my own judgment as to what I wish to do. Those who strongly believe I should live a certain way, are often times living lives contrary to what they preach. I wish to pass no judgment on others, for they have their own lives to live as they wish, as do I. I am merely using this example to show contradiction.

My conscience, Soul, that part of me that holds knowledge far beyond my capacity as human will be my guidance. No one knows better than I what the right or wrong choices are. I will be skeptical of those who claim to hold the truth for all and therefore all should follow their teachings. True teachers do not seek followers and do not try to impose their beliefs on others but simply share the knowledge they possess for everyone to benefit unconditionally.

I was not born to follow the desires of others, in fact, trying to satisfy others is an impossible task that will only bring me frustrations. Not only for myself but also for those trying to mold me into their own expectations as well.

I have a sort of "Jimmy, the cricket" on my shoulder, my own conscience, my own instincts as the best guidance system I could ever want. How I feel at any given time is the most accurate way for me to know if I am on the right path or I am not. I do not doubt the accuracy of my instincts for I believe they exist within me from a non-physical plane. I make little distinction between conscience, instinct and Soul because I see them as just a cluster of words that embody the same feeling of certainty. It is not all that beneficial to try and explain this concept for it is better felt than spoken. Through feeling, I believe is the only way I can experience this and an attempt to convey this feeling with words will only fall short.

Doubt arises from a history of contradictory beliefs I have gathered along the way. Many ideas and opinions of others have influenced and infected the pristine perfection I was when I was born, so I need to be diligent in identifying those instincts, those feelings that come from within. Whenever I feel doubt or apprehension in any given situation, it is usually a sign that lets me know that I should probably not do or say whatever I am about to. Whenever I feel I should not eat something for example, because I believe I wont feel well after doing so, it is very likely I will not feel well if I eat it. When I am in the process of negotiating a deal and I have a bad feeling about the experience, it probably means that this is not a transaction that will be favorable for me. When I meet someone and I get what is usually called "a bad vibe," I will most likely not have a positive interaction with that person. In short, I will pay attention to the signs I receive in all situations and then make a decision based on how I feel and then with great accuracy I will navigate through my experiences.

Money is not the enemy; there are many good people who are very wealthy. History is filled with them. Money is never the problem but my perception of it may be. I live in a society that is the most advanced in all of history, the accomplishments of the past fifty years alone are mind-blowing and things I could not even imagine are now a reality. I would dare to say that, without the economic system in which we live, none of these advances in technology we enjoy today could be.

There are many beautiful things created by very creative people that I would enjoy having, and I should feel no shame in the desiring of them, in fact, I should feel no shame at all in the desiring of anything since shame is a negative emotion and if I wish to live the life I intended to live, negative emotions are to be avoided.

I do not think twice about buying a television set, or a microwave oven or a pair of shoes, so why should it be any different for anything else? It seems once again that is a matter of perception. If I chose to buy an expensive car, I may feel guilty because perhaps I should have chosen a much less expensive one instead. I know they both will get me to the same destination, but why should I deprive myself of enjoying the best? My sacrifice will not benefit others and it will not benefit me. The purpose of life is to enjoy it. Who should define how I or anyone else should enjoy their lives? This is not being selfish because when I tend to my wellbeing first, I am benefiting myself as well as others. I would have little to give to others when I am not feeling well. In the end, I must come to the conclusion that I am not in this life to solve everyone's problems for they all have their own guidance systems and their own purposes in life of which I am not privy to. I will help others from a place of wellbeing and not from a feeling of guilt or any other social pressures, for this will not be beneficial to anyone. It is quite a journey the one I have embarked on, so I wish not to travel on someone else's.

Trying to decipher why I lack this or that, or why others have more or less than I do, is a recipe for more frustration. It is best to wish all well and try as best I can to live my life, the life I intended to. The life I am figuring out at every step and in this subject of money, just like in any other subject, it would be best if I let others figure out their path while I work on mine.

The way I feel about money determines my relationship with it. My financial wellbeing is depended upon the thoughts related to my economic situation. Whatever my economic situation is at this particular time it is closely linked to a pattern that I have develop over many years. No matter what the subject may be, money, relationships, physical health or any other, I will surrender myself to the belief that I have created every situation myself, either intentionally or unknowingly and from this moment on I will stop resisting and I will stop offering thoughts that are contrary to my desires. Since I believe this to be the case in my life, I can now make the necessary adjustments in the way I think and feel as to affect my future experiences and because everything begins at his moment in time, my former situation is now irrelevant. However, if I believe that nothing or very little will change because I am stuck in the past and my old patterns of thought are telling me that this is the way it has always been, there is then little if any room for improvement.

It is what I choose now that matters, the only thing that matters is the shift in consciousness I will implement at this time. I will not let former conditions and situations determine my future, in fact I will accept that the past was but a learning experience that has brought me to this point. A new point from where I now choose to create a better life. I will pay attention to the way I feel at this moment most of all and I will strive to feel the best way I can because I know that if I feel good in this moment and the moment after that and the one after, I can begin then to create heaven on earth. I can not stress strongly enough the importance of feeling good, it may seem superficial and simplistic, but it is the most effective way to affect all future conditions.

It is very likely I will fall back into old patterns of thought, for example when I go to the mailbox and find all sorts of bills I have to pay. I may be tempted to think that there is nothing I can do about them. I may think I am never going to get out of the hole. How can I shift my focus and create a new life when my present reality is telling me I am deep in debt? This is the pattern of thinking I was talking about and it only perpetuates my current situations and it is a reminder that I am fooling myself in believing that things could change. It is at this point that I must then begin my work.

I will put down the bills on the table, walk away and distract myself from those thoughts. I will tell myself that I will get to them later and when I come back to them I will pay them without allowing myself to create negative commentaries about it. I will tell myself that this bill will be paid off before I know it. The intent is not to fool myself into believing something that is not likely to happen but to soften my approach. I can try to perceive bills not as a nuisance but instead I may remember the things I bought and the joy they brought me at the time and have a different, more pleasant reaction.

If I have negative thoughts about money, I will only attract negative situations about money. I cannot receive the opposite of what I give out. So if my thoughts are about lack, or absence of money or if I recent others for having money, I cannot attract abundance. On the other hand, if I am glad others are doing well, if I am appreciative for the things that I do have, if I wish for others to do well, I will then begin to attract similar conditions to me. It is important that I give attention to good feeling thoughts for I will attract circumstances that will match those feelings. The better I feel around all circumstances, the faster the circumstances will shift more positively, no matter if the subject is health, happiness or money.

CHAPTER

10

"The Process"

As a fine artist, I have always struggled in enjoying what I did. I have asked myself many times, why am I experiencing frustration and rarely any enjoyment in my creations? I was even told once, "true artists do not enjoy their work, this is not a hobby for you", they would say, "this is pain, and suffering, and struggle, and frustration. You are pouring your heart into your work, and it is like a part of you is being torn onto the canvas", and I believed this for a long time. I thought true artists were troubled souls so this was what it must feel like. I strived so much for perfection that it was no wonder I felt such frustration. I was never happy with the process and many times I was not even pleased with the outcome no matter how wonderful others thought my work was. I know now that it is not because I am an artist but because I was troubled. My dissatisfaction with life was not just going to cease because of my art, but instead it was also going to be reflected in it.

I have heard those who say, "it is all about the journey, not the destination" or "I enjoy the process more than the end result." Wise words that did not mean much to me when the destination is where I wanted to be and the journey seemed like a burden. The process was not enjoyable for me since I wanted to rush and see the end result, just to find that once I was there and I had achieved my goal, it too was not gratifying in most cases.

My inability to be and enjoy the present moment where all of the joy and satisfaction is was the cause of my suffering. I know now that the enjoyment of the journey and the process is all captured within this one moment that is happening now and not later. It is in this place I am right now when everything happens and not in the future. When I speak of the journey and the pleasure I take in it, it is in the moment-by-moment experience I am having. When I speak of the joy of the process, I speak of the minute by minute I am involved in creation. Learning to be immersed in the moments that are evolving every second is joy.

When I pick up a brush and load it with the precious pigment that will eventually create the painting, the moment-by-moment strokes on the canvas are the inspiration, and seeing the evolution is the process that life is about. As I take pleasure in the application of the materials I see the results unfolding in real time. When I pay no mind to judgments that may surface and I allow the flow to continue, that is inspired work that comes from within, from spirit and therefore it is perfect.

The process is the same in every aspect of my life. It comes down to the vibration I offer through my emotions. The way I feel absolutely determines every outcome in every experience I have on this earth at all times.

The process is simple; I will find thoughts that please me. I will reach for thoughts that make me feel at ease with myself, I will find the thoughts that more easily bring me into a better feeling place. This means that I will strive to go with the flow and not be in a state of resistance. I will allow the wisdom of my inner being to guide me and I do that by paying attention to my emotions, paying attention to the way I feel. As I said before, my inner being lets me know when I need to adjust my thoughts through the way I feel.

The process is so simple that when I don't try to analyze things and turn them into a problem, it turns into an almost instinctive flowing event and with practice I look forward to living in this flow most of the time, leaving behind old patterns that do not serve me. I intend to be very conscious most of the time and stop allowing the "unconscious mind" to run my world. I believe the "unconscious mind" is nothing more than a storage space in my mind where all the positive and negative thoughts I have ever thought are gathered and through memory I allow them to surface.

The process as it relates to the subject of money

I will start in this moment to create a future of abundance for myself. It is my intention to see money as my friend and not my enemy, our relationship will be such that I will feel no lack because I have come into this lifetime experience to enjoy it and I believe that since this is a society where money plays an important role, I want to be a part of this society and not alienate myself from it. I want to live in harmony with all that is and material wealth is a component just as important as any other.

I understand that in order to attract wealth into my life, I need to have no negative feelings regarding this subject. Therefore, I will be happy for others who have achieved financial stability. I will look upon the financial success of others with admiration and I will feel much appreciation for the opportunities they provide for others. I will marvel at the advances of this generation and bless it with good feeling thoughts for in doing this I am contributing to the wellbeing of all. I do not use the word "bless" in a religious context as it is commonly used by others, but instead as a way to offer my best wishes.

It is a tremendous relief to be financially independent. To not have to worry about money is liberating. Much time and effort is wasted when I have to concern myself about having to pay this or that, worrying about how I am going to pay my bills next month. I know that once freed from these burdens, I am able to concentrate on other things that are probably more meaningful or important to me. But if I wait to be debt free, or financially independent to start doing those things, if I feel that not having enough money is what's keeping me from evolving and becoming that which I want to be or do, I am in fact putting obstacles in the path to financial independence. When I think about all of the things I could do if I had the money and feel bad or frustrated, I am not allowing money to flow in my direction, in fact the opposite is the case, any negativity I vibrate regarding this subject and in deed any other subject for that matter, I am without knowing, keeping the wealth I desire from coming. I must remember that what I resist persists. I am but a magnet that attracts everything that I think and feel, so if I feel negative about anything, I cannot attract positive outcomes.

I must emit good, positive vibrations in all aspects of my life so that the universe will then respond and bring to me the desired outcomes. Whatever my reasons for inviting financial wealth into my life are not a concern to the universe, the universe responds to what I feel. If the feeling of lack is what is present, the universe will bring me more of the same, if I feel good when I think about the things I want to have, if I rejoice in thoughts of winning the lottery and sharing my wealth with others, I am on the right path. This does not mean that I will win the lottery tomorrow, the key here is that I will feel good while thinking pleasant thoughts and in feeling good, the conditions will have to shift to match those feelings.

The process as it relates to the subject of relationships

There are many types of relationships I experience everyday and whatever those relationships are I want them to be good relationships. I want my interaction with others to be positive and uplifting. I want to enjoy the company of those people I choose to be around and I want them to enjoy their experiences with me as well.

There are many situations where an interaction with someone may feel unpleasant and since I want to avoid as many of those interactions as possible, the first thing I will do is prepare myself everyday by expressing feelings of appreciation and bringing myself to a place of peace and harmony. I can do this early in the morning when I wake up and bless myself and all that is around, offer appreciation for the good things in my life. I will meditate for fifteen minutes as to quiet my mind and then tell myself I would like to experience a good day and enjoy good exchanges with others.

As I do these things I am preparing myself by telling the universe what I would like and as long as I do not contradict my wishes with negative thoughts, the universe will gather the components that will make this day great. I will plan ahead and expect great outcomes. I will remember that I create my own life and if I am at ease and feeling good, the likelihood of having a good experience increases.

In any situations where I may find myself interacting with others, there is a chance that the exchange could turn negative, but the likelihood of that happening is slim. In such situation it is best if I can avoid the situation or remove myself from it. In the event I cannot do either I will use my thoughts to take me to a better feeling place. I will try not to judge the behaviors of others and I will refrain from having negative opinions or commentaries either spoken or in my head. I want to stay focused and not pollute my thinking in a way that will be detrimental to my positive state of mind.

When it comes to romantic relationships, I will always want to remind myself of the positive aspects of loved ones and pay little attention to things that may irritate me. When it comes to a relationship involving my partner, there may be times when less than pleasing situations will occur, but this will be temporary and can easily be resolved if I am in a place of love and appreciation.

Craving love in the absence of a partner can be a lonely experience but the more I pay attention to the absence of that partner I desire so much can only keep him or her away. I know that I can not dwell over negative situations and expect a desirable outcome so it is best if I wish for that loving partner and think of how beautiful it would feel to be together and in the experiencing of these emotions without a desperate desire for it to be, the wheels will begin to move me towards the love of my life.

The process as it relates to the subject of health

I came into this lifetime expecting to have perfect health. Over time, negative experiences and circumstances manifested as disease. What first were thoughts turned to beliefs and through the continued practice of negativity in one form or another, it finally developed into an undesirable physical illness. It is good for me to know this because it means I can do something about it, it means that I am not doomed to suffer forever but instead I can begin my recovery by applying the process.

As I mentioned before, I suffered for decades with many illnesses related to anxiety and depression, I was even given a label of Bipolar Disorder in my late forties. I can tell you now with certainty that I am not in the grip of any of these ailments. Through the process, I have been able to finally rid myself of the anguish that had me in bondage for so long, not to mention the negative effects my conditions had on loved ones.

Like mine, there are plenty of examples of people who have overcome even conditions that were deemed terminal by experts who refused to accept these are their destiny and found their way to full recovery. I understand that some who may be in terrible suffering will find this hard to believe, some will say that it is not possible to heal yourself and some may even be outraged at these claims, but if I am the sufferer of any illness and I feel sad, rage, guilt, despair or any other negative emotion, I am in fact adding fuel to the fire. Any and all negative emotions will only attract more and more unwanted things. I will instead encourage myself to do the process and allow it to work for me.

I will not speak nor will I engage in thinking about the condition I am suffering from. The more attention I give to it, the more I justify and attract undesirable outcomes. I will remember that because of The Law of Attraction I am a magnet and whatever vibration I offer I will draw more of the same to me.

I will go easy on myself, I will tell myself that Soul wants nothing but good for me. The universe will bring good health to me in time if I just relax as much as I can and distract myself with things that I enjoy. I will tell myself that this is a temporary situation and that in time I will feel better and better. I will do what feels right to me in my gut and I will not do what does not feel right because forcing myself to do something is going against the flow and it offers resistance and what I want to do most now is allow wellness in.

I will do breathing exercises and meditate. But mostly, I will find thoughts that feel good, I will create a good movie in my head for me to enjoy. I will try and go out in nature and pretend that everything is well because while pretending, while I am enjoying this movie I have created, I am offering nothing but positive vibrations and those vibrations will change my life.

The cells in my body change all the time, every so often these cells are replaced by new ones, so I will expect my body chemistry will be supportive of my idea on getting well. I will ask my body what it needs, this may sound crazy but just like with your inner being, we are having interactions with all that we are all the time whether we know it or not, so I would much rather do it intentionally.

I will discourage anyone from discontinuing to take his or her medications while doing the process. I certainly did not stop taking mine until I felt I could, I gradually sensed that I was in a place where I could begin to eliminate what I felt I no longer needed. I will also encourage anyone who feels they can do the same to do it under a doctor's supervision, pharmaceutical drugs are very powerful and they definitely alter the chemistry in my body so I would use extreme caution. I would encourage alternative medical practices for I believe they can be very effective in many cases.

CHAPTER 11

"The Teachers"

It is with much humility and great appreciation that I introduce the intelligence that has been a guiding light for me in this lifetime. Through my recollection of the life I have lived in this time-space, I will attempt to give you the names of those that have inspired me. Surely, I will forget many and perhaps even the names of those who have influenced the way I am today, however, since I believe the universe knows who they are, my thanks will reach even those not named here. I bless the kind Souls and all that is. Our connection in this lifetime, directly or indirectly affected us all and therefore a better world exists today because of it.

As a young child, my father who was an avid reader and who loved to study life even into his late years, introduced me to a poem by Rudyard Kipling titled "IF". The old and yellowed paper that it is today where my father typed this poem has since been framed and still hangs on my wall. This was I believe my first teaching.

Later as a young man, I came across a book titled, "The Road Less Traveled" by M. Scott Peck. A book I no longer remember its content but it somehow manages to appear in my mind as an influential piece of the puzzle of my life.

In my late twenties a coworker of mine told me how a book titled, "Many Lives, Many Masters" by Dr. Brian L. Weiss had changed his view on life and since then he no longer had the fear of dying. I subsequently went and bought the audiobook version of this book and found it to be a great revelation at the time, so much was the impact this book had on me that I decided to find this doctor. I knew that he would probably not take me as his patient since he now was a bestselling author but in any case, I thought I would try anyway.

I was blown away when I found out that his offices were within walking distance from the house I was living in at the time. Thrilled by this discovery, I called to make an appointment and I was told as I had suspected that the doctor was not seeing new patients but I was also told that there were other doctors in his office I could make an appointment with so I went ahead and scheduled my first appointment.

I met with one of the doctors and found that I could not successfully achieve the point of relaxation required for regression therapy. I was very disappointed but decided that I would try one of the other doctors. I thought that perhaps the chemistry I had with the first doctor was not great and I wanted a second opinion. Such was my desired to experience relief that I was not going to give up easily.

The second doctor was unsuccessful too in getting me to relax, so once again my attempt at regression therapy had failed. I decided then to give up on trying this method. Even though I was very discourage by what I believe was another failed attempt to finding a solution to the anxiety and depression I was experiencing I did not feel it was all a total loss, for the teachings I had found in this book stayed with me and I believe it was one of those candles I spoke of earlier that lit my path towards wellbeing.

I used to enjoy listening to audiobooks. I found no interest in reading because I could not concentrate, my eyes did not help much and at times reading would make me fall asleep and I would miss and forget pages I had already read and I would have to go back and reread them. The irony is that as a child I could easily read one book per day and I often did.

It was on this quest to listen to as many inspirational books I could find that I stumble upon the work of Dr. Wayne Dyer. I was so inspired by the sound of his soothing voice and the teaching that he spoke of that I was eager to listen to more and more of his work. I listened to many of his audiobooks, which lifted me up many of times and because of that Dr. Dyer was too, one who lit many candles along my path and I hope his Soul continues to guide me in an even more powerful way now that he is non-physical.

As life continued to unfold, my listening to audiobooks became intermittent so I would spend a lot of time away from these teaching that always seemed to inspire me and I would fall back into my usual life of disorganized thoughts, which always managed to push me off my path. It seemed like I tended to stay off the path more often than on it but the universe and my inner being would nudge me a little bit back into alignment every once in a while.

In one of these instances when I once again felt a desperate need of guidance I came upon a new audiobook titled, "The Power Of Now" by Eckhart Tolle. This book was at the time the most powerful candle that had ever been lit on my path. I heard these words that spoke to me so powerfully that I felt them within. I knew this knowledge I was being given was true. I understood it with such intensity that I would play this audiobook over and over again. I wanted to memorize this book. I felt that for the first time in my life I was in the presence of the life I had always wanted to live. This was the knowledge I had been searching for and even though I felt these words almost as my own, I had to keep hearing them constantly as to stay centered and focused on my path. I would tell others that if I could just live by the teachings of this book, my life would be perfect. I also found much inspiration listening to Dr. Deepak Chopra. I found his words to be very wise and they stimulated me in a very positive way.

Just like before though, my joy would not last long, even in the presence of what I thought was true wisdom my thoughts proved to be stronger and so I went off track once more. I have heard so many people say, "you needs to hit rock bottom before you can see the light." I felt that I would never see that light, that one last candle that would snap me out of all paths and onto a vast garden of peace.

What more would I need to experience? At times I even thought that my rock bottom would come in the form of a suicide attempt. The thoughts in my head struggle for answers, but all the while I still held hope. I now know that I do not need to struggle and I do not need a rock bottom to hit. This knowledge came to me from another teacher, or rather a group of teachers, and this time I was going to succeed.

I finally came upon the last candle a short time ago. There it was, Abraham, a group of non-physical beings that have been teaching the wisdom of the universe through a lovely woman named Esther. I cannot express in words my deep appreciation for Jerry and Esther Hicks who so kindly have share the teaching of Abraham through their books. To you, Abraham, my most sincere thanks.

I have always been skeptical and I must say I have also felt fearful of the metaphysical world. I was not one to want to explore spirituality in this manner; I was more inclined to a Buddhist sort of approach. Not that I had much knowledge about Buddhism either but the peaceful appearance of those who practiced it felt inspiring to me.

I had been aware of those beings in non-physical form that communicate with others in the physical world through mediums as in the cases presented by Dr. Brian L. Weiss in his book, Many Lives, Many Masters and others but it never felt personal to me. It seemed less specific and perhaps even vague, but not this time.

Abraham teachings felt directed at me personally. This time I felt I was being given specific, no-nonsense wisdom that could be practiced and put to the test. I understood clearly and I felt strongly that this knowledge would free me once and for all from my stubborn afflictions and here I am. The teachings of Abraham are the reason I am well today and the source of my inspiration to write this book.

I believe that we are all teachers and we are all students as well. I believe that every interaction we have with one another is a learning experience. I would like to express my most heartfelt appreciation to all, everyone who has come into my path.

Epilogue

I want to share with the readers some of the work I have done as an fine artist. I have chosen to illustrate this book with images of my paintings of dog portraits I have created for clients, collectors and for myself. I find quite an enjoyment in seeing the expressive faces that inspire such good feelings.

These amazing being are a pure example of unconditional love and appreciation. There is much we can learn from just being around them and looking into their eyes. It is no wonder that dogs are used as a form of therapy in many hospitals as well as the help they offer many with disabilities. The healing power that is the feeling good in the presence of these amazing creatures is a true statement to the goodness there is in the universe. If we were to learn to be in the present moment as our dogs are, it would be a blessing.

There is much in nature that can teach us what life is all about. There is no rush in a flower to open its bloom, there is no frustration in the stream as the water hits the rock for it simply goes around it and there is no anxious thought in the caterpillar to become a butterfly. Nature just seems to adjust and adapt naturally without effort.

If only we would trust in the universe and believe that it too takes care of us as it does nature and all we need to do is let go and allow the natural flow of life to happen without interfering with our resistant thoughts, we would realize how magical it all is.

Dog Portrait
Paintings

artcotera.com

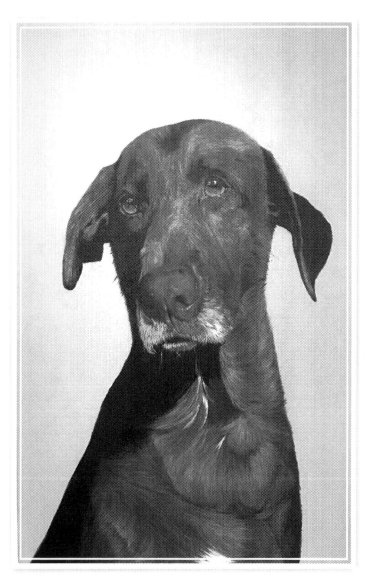

artcotera.com

artcotera.com

artcotera.com

artcotera.com

artcotera.com

artcotera.com

Printed in the United States
By Bookmasters